AF263983

Systematic Theology Workbook 5-in-1

Guided Exercises, Reflections, and Study Questions on God, Humanity, Salvation, the Spirit, and the Future

TABLE OF CONTENTS

INTRODUCTION

This 5-in-1 workbook is for Christians who want a steady, Bible-shaped faith. It is for people who want to know what they believe, why they believe it, and how to live it out with a clear mind and a faithful heart. Many believers love God, yet feel unsure when hard questions come. Some have pieces of truth, but the pieces do not connect. This collection helps you put those pieces together, using Scripture as the foundation.

Systematic theology means gathering what the whole Bible teaches about key topics and holding those truths side by side. It is not about winning arguments. It is about learning to think God's thoughts after Him, as best we can, with humility. Clear doctrine protects your joy. It guards you from errors that sound kind but pull you away from truth. It also strengthens your worship, because you praise God more truly when you see Him more clearly.

This series is a workbook on purpose. Many books explain ideas but never help you practice them. Here, each chapter gives a short teaching section in plain language. Then it gives guided exercises that help the truth move from your head to your life. You will read, write, reflect, and pray. You will also be asked to connect doctrine to daily choices, relationships, and habits. That is where growth becomes real.

You can expect a steady pattern in every chapter. First, you will get a focused lesson that stays on one theme. It will not wander. It will use Scripture carefully and avoid filler. Then you will move into a workbook section. That section includes study questions, space for your own words, and prompts that call for honest self-examination. You will also find short prayer starters. These are meant to help you respond to God with reverence and trust.

This collection is arranged as five short books, each with six chapters. Each book covers one major area of Christian doctrine.

Book One helps you know God as He has revealed Himself. You will study His self-revelation, the Trinity, His rule over all things, His moral goodness, His relationship with time, and the call to worship Him in truth.

Book Two focuses on humanity. You will study what it means to be made in God's image, why human life has worth, what sin is, what the fall has done to us, and how we should live as image-bearers in a broken world.

Book Three focuses on salvation. You will study God's grace, the work of Christ, the call to faith and repentance, justification, growth in holiness, and the steady hope God gives to those who belong to Him.

Book Four focuses on the Holy Spirit. You will study who the Spirit is, how He gives life, how He unites believers to Christ, how He shapes character, how He works in the church, and what it looks like to walk in daily dependence on Him.

Book Five focuses on the future. You will study the return of Christ, resurrection, judgment, the final state, and how Christian hope shapes faithful living right now.

Each book builds on the last. You will see how the doctrines connect. What you learn about God shapes how you understand yourself. What you learn about humanity shapes why salvation is needed. What you learn about salvation shapes how you depend on the Spirit. What you learn about the Spirit shapes how you wait for the future with steady hope.

What will you gain if you work through this collection with care?

You can gain a clearer view of God's character. Many fears shrink when God's greatness becomes more real to you. You can gain stronger confidence in Scripture, because you will practice handling key passages with attention and respect. You can gain better discernment, because you will learn to test ideas against biblical truth. You can gain a steadier prayer life, because your prayers will be shaped by what God has revealed. You can gain greater humility, because theology done well reminds us we are creatures, not the Creator. You can also gain a stronger sense of purpose, because doctrine connects belief to obedience.

You can also expect to grow in your ability to explain your faith with clarity. Some believers want to share Christ but feel stuck when questions come. Others have the right words but struggle to speak with gentleness. This workbook helps you practice simple explanations, using careful language. Scripture calls believers to be ready to give a reason for the hope within them, with gentleness and respect (1 Peter 3:15, NSV). This study helps you move in that direction.

This workbook is also meant to help you notice what you already assume. Everyone has beliefs, even if they have never written them down. Some beliefs came from family. Some came from church culture. Some came from pain. Some came from social media. Over time, people can collect ideas that do not fit together. This can cause confusion and doubt. When you study doctrine in an ordered way, you begin to see what is true, what is uncertain, and what needs to change. That is a gift from God.

Here is how to use this workbook well

First, take it slow. The goal is not speed. The goal is depth and obedience. Plan a steady pace you can keep. Many people do well with one chapter per week. That gives time to read, write, pray, and revisit key ideas.

Second, keep your Bible open. Do not treat the teaching section as the final word. It is a guide, not a replacement for Scripture. Look up each passage. Read the surrounding verses when you can. Note repeated words. Note what the text says and what it does not say. A wise habit is to write the main point of each passage in one sentence, using your own words.

Third, write your answers. You may feel tempted to think through the questions without writing. Writing slows you down in a good way. It helps you notice what you really believe. It also gives you a record you can review later. Over time, you will see growth. You will also see patterns in your struggles and prayers. Those patterns can help you seek counsel and make changes.

Fourth, be honest. Some questions will reveal fears, doubts, or sins you would rather avoid. Do not hide from those moments. Bring them into the light before God. He already knows your heart. The goal is not to look strong. The goal is to become steady in faith.

Fifth, use this with others if you can. You can work through it with a friend, a spouse, a small group, or a class. When believers study together, they often see things they would miss alone. You can also sharpen one another through respectful conversation. If you do it as a group, set a simple plan. Read the teaching section beforehand. Then discuss the questions and share what you learned. Keep the tone humble. Stay close to Scripture. Pray at the end.

You may wonder if theology will make your faith dry. It does not have to. Theology becomes dry when it is separated from worship and obedience. But when theology is rooted in Scripture and applied to life, it becomes a source of strength. It helps you endure suffering. It helps you resist temptation. It helps you forgive others. It helps you face death with hope. It helps you worship with understanding.

Many people feel tossed around by constant opinions. One week they feel sure. The next week they feel lost. The Bible calls believers to maturity, so they are not carried by every changing wind of teaching. A steady grasp of core doctrine is part of that maturity.

You will also notice that this workbook avoids unnecessary arguments. Christians do not agree on every detail in every area. Some topics have faithful believers on more than one side. When that happens, this workbook will focus on what Scripture clearly teaches, and it will keep the main things central. The goal is not to start fights. The goal is to build faithfulness.

You will see that each chapter includes application. Doctrine without application becomes pride. Application without doctrine becomes confusion. God gives truth so we can live in truth. This workbook presses that connection again and again. If you learn a truth about God, you will be asked how it changes your worship. If you learn a truth about sin, you will be asked how it changes your confession and choices. If you learn a truth about salvation, you will be asked how it changes your gratitude and obedience.

Expect some conviction. That is normal. Expect some comfort too. God's truth both exposes and heals. It calls you to repent, and it calls you to trust God's grace. It also gives you language for prayer when your own words feel small.

This collection is also meant to be revisited. You might work through it once, then return later at a slower pace. Or you might use one book during a season of study, then use a different book when new questions arise. Each section stands on its own, but the whole set works best when read in order.

One last encouragement

Ask God to teach you as you study. If you belong to Christ, you are not alone in this work. God uses His Word to shape His people. As you read and write, you are practicing listening. You are training your mind and heart to submit to truth. Over time, that kind of practice bears fruit.

As you begin, keep your aim simple. Know God more truly. Trust Him more deeply. Obey Him more fully. Then teach others what you learn, with patience and love. This workbook is here to help you do just that.

BOOK ONE
KNOW GOD AS HE HAS REVEALED HIMSELF

We do not make guesses about who God is. We listen to what He has said. God reveals Himself through His Word, and that is where we begin. This book focuses on how God has made Himself known: His name, His character, His rule, and His call to worship Him in truth. Each chapter gives Scripture-based teaching and space to reflect and respond. These truths are not for head knowledge alone. They shape how we live, pray, and worship. The goal is simple: to know the true God and respond to Him with faith.

CHAPTER 1

START WITH GOD'S SELF-DISCLOSURE

If we want to know God, we must start with how He has spoken. God is not silent. He has shown who He is through creation, through Scripture, and most clearly through His Son. We do not define Him. He defines Himself.

God told Moses His name at the burning bush: **"I AM WHO I AM"** (Exodus 3:14, NSV). This simple phrase speaks volumes. God depends on no one. He has no beginning or end. He exists in Himself. He is not like us. He does not change. He does not grow. He is always present, always holy, always true.

In the Bible, names often show character. God gives Himself many names, each revealing part of who He is. He is **El Elyon** (God Most High), **El Shaddai** (God Almighty), **Yahweh** (the LORD), and **Jehovah-Jireh** (the LORD Will Provide). These are not just titles. They are truths about His nature and how He acts.

Psalm 19:1 says, **"The heavens declare the glory of God"**. Nature shows His greatness, but nature cannot tell us everything. To know God's heart, His will, and His plan for us, we need His Word. Scripture is not just information. It is revelation. It tells us what He wants us to know. And it does not change with time or culture.

Hebrews 1:1–2 says God once spoke through the prophets, but now speaks through His Son. Jesus is the perfect image of God. When we see Christ, we see God with skin on. He shows us God's mercy, power, and truth in human form.

God's self-disclosure is always clear, but we often don't want to hear it. Romans 1:19–21 says that people suppress the truth. Even though God has made Himself known, many reject Him. They trade His glory for empty idols. But those who listen, believe, and submit find life.

Knowing God is not like reading a textbook. It is personal. It calls for humility. We don't come with answers. We come to receive. And what we receive is truth that brings light. We do not figure God out. He makes Himself known, and we respond in worship.

Here is the main idea: God wants to be known. That is why He speaks. That is why He gave us His Word. That is why He sent His Son. And that is why we begin this study not by asking who we think God is, but by asking: What has God said about Himself?

Workbook Section

Read and Reflect

Read these Scriptures carefully. What do they say about how God reveals Himself?

- Exodus 3:13–15

  ____

  ____

- Psalm 19:1–4

  ____

  ____

- Romans 1:18–23

  ____

  ____

- Hebrews 1:1–3

  ____

  ____

Write down one phrase from each passage that stood out to you:

1. Exodus 3: ____

   ____

2. Psalm 19: ____

   ____

3. Romans 1: ____

   ____

4. Hebrews 1: ____

____

Now answer these reflection questions:

1. In what ways has God already made Himself known to you through Scripture or life experience?

____

____

____

____

2. Why do you think people often ignore or reject what God has revealed?

____

____

____

____

3. Which of God's names means the most to you right now, and why?

____

____

____

____

____

Personal Application

1. God has revealed Himself in specific ways. Which one (creation, Scripture, or Christ) do you want to focus on more in your life this week?

____

____

____

Hebrews 1: ____

____

____

2. How can you build a habit of listening to God's Word instead of
   your own ideas about Him?

   ----

3. Write out a short response to God, based on what you learned.

Prayer Response

"Father, thank You for speaking. Thank You for showing who You are. Help me to trust what You say. Teach me to listen. Teach me to worship You for who You are, not who I imagine. Amen."

Key Takeaway

God does not leave us guessing. He speaks. His Word tells us who He is. Our job is to listen and believe.

CHAPTER 2

SEE GOD AS TRINITY: ONE IN THREE

God is one. This is clear from Scripture. But within that oneness, He has revealed Himself as three persons: the Father, the Son, and the Holy Spirit. Each is fully God. Each is distinct. Yet there is only one God.

This is not a human idea. It is not a problem to solve. It is a truth to receive. God shows this clearly in His Word, beginning in the Old Testament. In Genesis 1:26, God says, **"Let us make man in our image."** He speaks as more than one, yet He acts as one. Later, in Isaiah 48:16, the speaker says, **"The Lord GOD has sent Me, and His Spirit."** One sentence. Three persons.

In the New Testament, the Trinity is even clearer. At Jesus' baptism in Matthew 3:16–17, the Son is baptized, the Spirit descends like a dove, and the Father speaks from heaven. All three are present. All three are active.

Jesus also speaks of the Trinity when He tells His disciples to baptize **"in the name of the Father and of the Son and of the Holy Spirit"** (Matthew 28:19). Notice that the word "name" is singular. One name. Three persons.

The Father is not the Son. The Son is not the Spirit. The Spirit is not the Father. But each is fully God. They are equal in power and nature, but they relate to each other in order. The Father sends the Son. The Son sends the Spirit. They work in unity and never oppose each other.

Some try to explain the Trinity using images like water, clover, or an egg. These are all limited and often lead to wrong ideas. God is not like anything else. He is unique. We must let Scripture lead, even when our minds feel stretched.

The Trinity is not a side point. It is central. Salvation, prayer, and worship all involve the whole Trinity. The Father planned salvation. The Son accomplished it. The Spirit applies it to our hearts. We pray to the Father, through the Son, by the Spirit. We worship one God who is Father, Son, and Spirit.

Why does this matter? Because it shows us that God is complete in Himself. Before the world was made, the Father loved the Son through the Spirit. God did not create us because He was lonely. He created us to reflect His joy and love.

The Trinity also shows how unity and difference can exist together in perfect peace. In a world filled with division, God shows us what perfect love and unity look like. This shapes how we live, how we treat others, and how we serve in the church.

God is not like us. But He has shown enough of Himself that we can know Him truly, even if not fully. We cannot explain the Trinity in full, but we can believe it, because this is what God has said.

Workbook Section

Read and Reflect

Read each passage and write a short summary of what it reveals about the Trinity.

1. Genesis 1:26

    ____

    ____

2. Isaiah 48:16

    ____

    ____

3. Matthew 3:16–17

    ____

    ____

4. Matthew 28:19

    ____

    ____

5. John 14:26

What do these verses teach you about the relationship between the Father, Son, and Spirit?

Why is it important that each person of the Trinity is fully God?

How does the truth of the Trinity affect how you think about God's love?

1. In prayer, we often focus on one person of the Trinity. How can you begin to speak to the Father, thank the Son, and depend on the Spirit in your prayers?

2. How can the unity within the Trinity shape how you treat others in your family, church, or work?

----

3. Do you struggle with this truth? If so, what holds you back? If not, what helps you rest in it?

Key Takeaway

God is one in nature, three in person. The Father, Son, and Spirit are not separate gods. They are one God. This truth leads us to worship with awe and humility.

Prayer Response

Father, thank You for revealing Yourself as one God in three persons. Thank You for sending the Son to save me and the Spirit to live in me. Help me to trust what You have said, even when I do not fully understand. Help me live in unity with others as You live in perfect unity forever. Amen.

CHAPTER 3

RECOGNIZE GOD'S SOVEREIGNTY IN ALL THINGS

God is sovereign. This means He reigns over everything, everywhere, all the time. His rule is not limited to certain places or moments. He is never caught off guard, never confused, never overruled. There is no one higher than God, no one stronger, no one wiser.

Psalm 103:19 says, **"The Lord has established His throne in the heavens, and His kingdom rules over all."** His rule is not just a claim—it is a fact. Everything that exists is under His authority, including time, space, nature, rulers, angels, and every human life.

When we say God is sovereign, we mean three things:

1. **God has the right to rule all things.** He made everything. He owns everything. As Creator, He alone has full authority.

2. **God has the power to rule all things.** Nothing can stop Him. He does not need help or permission.

3. **God is actively ruling all things.** He is not passive. He is not distant. He is involved at every level: personal, global, and eternal.

We see God's sovereignty clearly in creation. Genesis 1 shows that He speaks and things happen. Light appears. Land separates from sea. Stars fill the sky. Living creatures fill the earth. Nothing resists Him. Nature listens.

God's rule is not only over nature but also over history. He guided Israel out of Egypt. He chose leaders. He removed kings. He used both faithful and wicked people to accomplish His plans. Proverbs 21:1 says, **"The king's heart is a stream of water in the hand of the Lord; He turns it wherever He will."**

God's rule also extends to nations. Daniel 2:21 says He **"changes times and seasons; He removes kings and sets up kings."** Nations rise and fall, not by chance, but by His hand.

But God's sovereignty is not just big, it is also close. Jesus said that not even a sparrow falls to the ground apart from God, and that every hair on your head is numbered (Matthew 10:29–30). This means God is deeply aware and involved in the smallest parts of your life. He knows your steps. He knows your needs. He knows your tears.

Still, many people struggle with this truth. They ask, "If God is in control, why is the world so broken?" That's an honest question. The Bible gives us a full view: God is not the author of evil, but He is never overpowered by it. He allows sin for a time, but He limits it. And He uses even pain and loss for good in the lives of those who love Him (Romans 8:28). Evil never gets the final word, God does.

This is also true in salvation. God is sovereign in choosing, calling, and saving His people. Ephesians 1:4–5 says God chose us in Christ before the world began. He planned to adopt us through Jesus Christ. He is not waiting to see who will come to Him. He draws people to Himself by grace.

Romans 8:30 says, **"Those whom He predestined He also called, and those whom He called He also justified, and those whom He justified He also glorified."** From beginning to end, salvation is God's work. This does not cancel our responsibility. We must believe and repent. But even our faith is a gift He gives.

Some people fear this truth. But if God were not in control, we could not trust Him. If He had limits, He would not be worthy of worship. God's control is not meant to scare us; it is meant to settle us. He is not reckless. He is wise, good, and just in all He does.

When we truly believe God is sovereign, we can rest. We do not have to carry every burden or solve every problem. We can trust that His plans are better than our own, even when we do not see the full picture.

This also affects how we respond to suffering. Pain is real. Loss is hard. But nothing is wasted in God's hands. Joseph told his brothers in Genesis 50:20, **"You meant evil against me, but God meant it for good."** That's not a weak hope. It's a strong truth. God rules over both joy and sorrow, and He brings good even from what others mean for harm.

So how do we live under God's rule?

- We trust Him when life is uncertain.
- We obey Him, knowing He sees everything.
- We pray to Him, because He has the power to act.
- We worship Him, because He deserves all glory.

God's sovereignty is not cold. It is personal. He is not only in charge, He is present. He is not only strong, He is good. And He is not only above all—He is near to all who call on Him.

Read and Reflect

Read the verses below. Write one truth you see in each:

1. Psalm 103:19

   ____

   ____

2. Proverbs 21:1

   ____

   ____

3. Daniel 2:21

   ____

   ____

4. Matthew 10:29–30

   ____

   ____

5. Romans 8:28–30

   ____

   ____

6. Genesis 50:20

   ____

   ____

1. How does knowing God rules all things change how you view your current season of life?

   ----

2. Think of a time when a plan you made did not work out. Looking back, how might God have used that for your growth?

   ----

3. Do you struggle with trusting God's control over your future? Why or why not?

Personal Application

A. Resting in God's Rule

Write down one area of your life where you tend to take control or feel anxious. What would it look like to trust God's rule in that area?

B. Praying Under God's Sovereignty

When you pray, do you truly believe God has the power to act? Why does trusting His rule change the way you pray?

C. Living with Purpose

If God is in control of every part of life, how does that give meaning to even the small tasks in your day?

Key Takeaway

God is not just in control of the universe, He is in control of your life. He does not forget, overlook, or lose sight of anything. His rule brings peace, purpose, and hope.

Prayer Response

Father, You are Lord over all things, past, present, and future. I praise You for ruling with wisdom, not confusion. With purpose, not chance. With love, not distance. Help me surrender my fear, my plans, and my will. Teach me to rest in Your rule and trust that You never fail. In Jesus' name, Amen.

CHAPTER 4

TRUST GOD'S MORAL GOODNESS

Many people believe God is powerful. Fewer believe He is good. Some carry fears about God that come from pain, harsh leaders, or broken homes. Others assume God is like a stricter version of themselves. Scripture corrects all of that. God is morally perfect. He is pure. He is just. He is faithful. And He never acts with sin or blame.

Deuteronomy 32:4 says, "All his ways are justice." That means God never does wrong. He never bends truth. He never takes a bribe. He never plays favorites. He never lies to get His way. His goodness is not a mood. It is part of who He is.

God's goodness includes His holiness. Holiness means God is set apart from all evil. He is completely clean. Isaiah 6:3 calls Him holy. This is not a small detail. If God were not holy, He could not be trusted. A god who can tolerate sin without care is not good. He is unsafe.

God's goodness also includes His justice. Psalm 89:14 says righteousness and justice are the foundation of His throne. God's rule is not random. He does not judge based on opinions. He judges based on truth. He calls sin what it is. He hates what destroys His creation and harms His people. His justice is good news because it means evil will not last forever.

But God's moral goodness is not only justice. It also includes mercy. Mercy means God shows compassion to people who deserve judgment. He does not ignore sin, but He is patient with sinners. Romans 2:4 speaks of God's kindness and patience leading people to repentance. God is not eager to crush. He is eager to save. His patience is not weakness. It is strength under control.

Some people struggle to hold these truths together. They think God must be either loving or just. Scripture says He is both. He does not choose between them. He is not split inside. He is one God, with one perfect character.

Here is a simple way to think about it. God's love means He does good to others. God's justice means He does what is right. God's mercy means He helps the helpless. God's wrath means He opposes evil. Wrath is not God losing control. Wrath is His settled opposition to sin. A good judge must hate what is evil. If God did not oppose sin, He would not be morally good.

James 1:17 says every good gift is from God. This shows another part of His goodness. God is generous. He gives life, breath, daily bread, strength, and help. Many of His gifts come to people who do not thank Him. That is kindness. It is also a call to repentance.

So what does it mean to trust God's moral goodness?

First, it means you let God define good and evil. We live in a time when people rename sin as freedom and call selfishness a right. Scripture calls us to submit our moral judgment to God's Word. Micah 6:8 says God has told us what is good. God does not hide His standards. He makes them known.

Second, trusting God's goodness means you stop measuring God by your comfort. God may lead you through hard days. Hard does not mean evil. Discipline does not mean hate. Correction does not mean rejection. God can be good and still allow hardship for a wise purpose.

Third, trusting God's goodness means you obey even when it costs you. Many sins look pleasant for a moment. Many acts of obedience feel costly at first. But God's commands are not traps. They are good paths. They protect you, shape you, and point you toward life.

Fourth, trusting God's goodness means you repent with hope. When God exposes sin, He is not trying to destroy you. He is calling you back. His goodness invites you to return to Him. His mercy gives room to confess. His justice makes forgiveness meaningful. His holiness makes change possible.

If you want a steady faith, you must settle this truth in your heart. God is morally good. He is never cruel. He is never unfair. He is never careless. When you do not understand His ways, you can still trust His character. That trust becomes a strong anchor in both joy and suffering.

Workbook Section

Scripture Study

Read each passage. Then write one sentence that explains what it shows about God's moral goodness.

1. Deuteronomy 32:4

    ----

2. Psalm 89:14

    ----

3. Romans 2:4

    ----

4. James 1:17

    ----

5. Micah 6:8

    ----

6. Isaiah 6:3

Clear Thinking Exercise

Write short answers. Use your own words.

1. What is the difference between God's justice and God's mercy?

    ----

2. Why is God's holiness good news, not bad news?

----

3. What is one common lie people believe about God's goodness?

Heart Check

Choose one area. Be honest and specific.

1. Where do you most doubt God's goodness right now?

   Examples: your past, your health, your finances, your family, your unanswered prayers.

   ----

2. What have you been tempted to believe about God because of that struggle?

   ----

3. Based on the passages you read, what is true about God's character in this area?

Pick one command of God that you find hard to follow. Keep it concrete.

1. The command I struggle with is:

   ----

2. Why it feels hard:

   ----

3. One small act of obedience I will do in the next 48 hours:

   ----

4. One person who can support me in this:

Prayer Response

Write a short prayer of trust. Use your own words. If you get stuck, start with these lines and finish them.

Father, You are holy and You do what is right.

I confess that I have doubted Your goodness when ____.

Help me believe what Your Word says about You.

Teach me to obey You in ____.

Thank You for Your kindness that leads me to repentance.

Amen.

Key Takeaway

God's moral goodness is steady. He is holy, just, and merciful. When you cannot trace His plan, you can trust His character.

CHAPTER 5

UNDERSTAND GOD'S RELATIONSHIP WITH TIME

People live inside time. We count minutes. We feel hurry. We regret the past and worry about the future. God is not like that. He made time, so He is not trapped by it. Scripture shows that God is eternal. He has no beginning and no end. He does not learn new facts. He does not get older. He does not run out of time.

Psalm 90:2 says, "From everlasting to everlasting you are God." God's life has no edges. He is not a long-lived creature. He is the Creator who always is.

God's relationship with time helps us trust Him. We change. Our feelings shift. Our plans fail. God does not change. Malachi 3:6 says, "I the Lord do not change." His promises stay sure. His character stays clean. His purpose stays steady.

God also sees the full story at once. We see one page. God sees the whole book. Isaiah 46:10 says God declares the end from the beginning. This does not mean God guesses well. It means He knows and rules over what will happen. Nothing takes Him by surprise.

This truth is meant to calm us, not confuse us. God is not rushed. He is never late. He is never early. He works with perfect wisdom. 2 Peter 3:8 reminds us that God's sense of time is not like ours. What feels slow to us is not slow to Him. He is patient and purposeful.

God's eternal nature also means He is always faithful in every season. When you feel stuck, God is not stuck. When you feel like time is running out, God is not anxious. When you feel like your past has ruined you, God is still able to redeem. When you fear the future, God is already there.

Still, God works within time. He acts in real history. He gives days and years. He sets seasons. Ecclesiastes 3:1 says there is a time for every matter under heaven. That verse does not mean every moment is pleasant. It means life has rhythms, and God is not absent from them.

God gives time as a gift and a responsibility. Ephesians 5:15–16 tells believers to walk wisely and make the best use of time. That means time matters. We cannot get it back. God calls us to use it well.

So how should we live in light of God's relationship with time?

First, live with steady trust. If God is eternal and unchanging, you do not need to panic when life shifts. You can make plans, but you do not need to cling to them. Proverbs 16:9 says a person plans his way, but the Lord directs his steps. You can hold your plans with open hands.

Second, practice patient obedience. Many people want fast answers. But God often grows His people slowly. Waiting is not wasted time when it is done with faith. God uses waiting to shape character, deepen prayer, and expose idols.

Third, repent quickly. Time is limited for us. James 4:14 says our life is like a mist. That is not meant to scare you. It is meant to wake you up. Do not delay obedience. Do not delay confession. Do not delay seeking peace with others.

Fourth, live with hope. Because God is Lord of time, history is going somewhere. God is not reacting to events. He is carrying out His purpose. The future is not empty. It is held by God.

When you understand God's relationship with time, you can rest. You can also work. You rest because God is steady. You work because your days matter. The goal is not to control time. The goal is to trust the One who holds it.

Workbook Section

Scripture Study

Read each passage. Then write one sentence about what it teaches about God and time.

1. Psalm 90:2

----

2. Malachi 3:6

____

____

3. Isaiah 46:10

____

____

4. 2 Peter 3:8

____

____

5. Ecclesiastes 3:1

____

____

6. James 4:14

____

____

Connect the Truth

Answer in your own words.

1. What is the difference between God being eternal and God being simply "very old"?

____

____

____

____

____

2. Why does God's unchanging nature matter for His promises?

____

____

____

____

3. What happens to your faith when you measure God's work by
    your timeline?

Time Audit

Write down how you used your time yesterday. Keep it simple and
honest.

Morning: ____

____

Midday: ____

____

Evening: ____

____

Now answer:

1. What part of your day showed wise use of time?

    ----

2. What part of your day felt wasted or careless?

    ----

3. What is one change you can make this week that would honor
    God?

Think of one area where you are waiting on God.

I am waiting for:

What I fear while waiting:

What I can do while waiting:

Now write one sentence of trust based on Isaiah 46:10.

Repent and Act

Choose one area where you have delayed obedience.

The obedience I have delayed is:

Why I have delayed it:

One step I will take in the next 24 hours:

Write a short prayer. If you need help, begin with these lines and finish them.

Lord, You are eternal and You never change.

____

____

Help me stop rushing and start trusting You in _________________ .

____

Teach me to use my time wisely by ________________________ .

____

Give me patience to obey while I wait for ____________________ .

____

Thank You that You hold my past, my present, and my future.

____

____

Amen.

God is eternal and unchanging. He is never rushed and never late. Your time is limited, so use it wisely and trust the God who holds every day.

CHAPTER 6

WORSHIP GOD IN TRUTH

Worship is not a style. Worship is a response to God. It is giving Him the honor He deserves because of who He is and what He has done. True worship begins with truth, not preference. If we worship a version of God we made up, we are not worshiping God. We are worshiping an idea.

Jesus said, "The true worshipers will worship the Father in spirit and truth" (John 4:23, NSV). Truth matters because God is real. He has revealed Himself. He tells us what pleases Him. Worship is not a place you go once a week. It is a life of reverence and obedience that flows from a heart made alive by God.

Worship includes singing, prayer, and hearing Scripture, but it does not stop there. Romans 12:1 calls believers to present their bodies as a living sacrifice. That is worship. When you obey God in private, that is worship. When you forgive, speak truth, and turn from sin, that is worship. When you serve others with love, that is worship.

Truth-shaped worship also means we approach God the way He tells us to. Nadab and Abihu offered unauthorized fire and faced judgment (Leviticus 10:1–3). That account is sobering, but it teaches a lasting lesson. God is not to be treated lightly. He is holy. We do not set the terms. He does.

That does not mean worship should be joyless. God is worthy of gladness and gratitude. Psalm 100:2 calls people to serve the Lord with gladness. But gladness must be guided by truth. Real joy grows when we see God clearly, not when we chase a feeling.

Worship in truth also requires right thinking about God. If you think God is small, your worship will be small. If you think God is harsh, you will either hide from Him or try to earn His favor. If you think God does not care about sin, you will treat sin as a minor issue. But when you see God as He is, worship becomes steady and sincere.

God also cares about the heart. Isaiah 29:13 warns about honoring God with lips while the heart is far away. God does not want empty words. He wants a real response. This is why confession matters. You cannot cling to sin and worship God in truth at the same time. Psalm 24:3-4 asks who may stand in God's holy place. The answer includes clean hands and a pure heart. This is not perfection. It is honesty, repentance, and a desire to obey.

Worship in truth shapes how we live together as the church. Scripture calls believers to build one another up, to let the Word of Christ dwell richly, and to sing with gratitude. In true worship, God stays central. The focus is not the crowd, the mood, or the platform. The focus is God's glory and the good of His people.

So how do you worship God in truth?

Start with Scripture. Let God's Word set your view of Him. Then respond with prayer and praise. Confess sin quickly. Give thanks for real gifts. Obey what God has said. Serve others in love. These things are not separate from worship. They are worship.

Worship in truth also prepares you for hard days. When life is painful, feelings can swing. But truth does not move. If your worship is built on truth, you can keep honoring God even when you are tired, confused, or sad. You may not feel strong, but you can still be faithful.

God is worthy of worship in every season. He is worthy when you understand and when you do not. He is worthy when life is full and when life is empty. Worship in truth is a steady offering of trust, reverence, and obedience to the living God.

Scripture Study

Read each passage. Then write one sentence about what it teaches you about worship.

1. John 4:23

    ----

2. Romans 12:1

    ----

3. Leviticus 10:1–3

    ----

4. Psalm 100:2

    ----

5. Isaiah 29:13

    ----

6. Psalm 24:3–4

Worship Check

Answer honestly.

1. When you think of worship, what do you usually picture?

    ----

2. Which is harder for you, worshiping with joy or worshiping with reverence? Why?

----

3. What tends to distract your heart during worship gatherings or private prayer?

Truth Before Feeling

Write a short list of true statements about God that can guide your worship even when feelings are low.

1. God is:

----

2. God has:

----

3. God will:

Now write one sentence explaining how these truths help you worship when life is hard.

Living Worship Plan

Pick one action you will take this week to worship God in truth.
Choose one:

- Daily Scripture reading for 10 minutes

- Confession and repentance in one specific area

- Serving someone quietly without being noticed

- Giving thanks for three specific gifts each day

- Setting aside one hour for prayer and reflection

My choice:

My plan for when and how I will do it:

Repair the Heart

Isaiah 29:13 warns about worship with words but not the heart. Write a short confession if your heart has been distant.

What has pulled my heart away:

What I need to repent of:

What I will change this week:

Prayer Response

Write a prayer in your own words. If you need help, start here and finish it.

Father, You are worthy of honor and praise.

Forgive me for treating worship as ________________________ .

Teach me to worship You in spirit and truth by ________________

-- .

Help my life match my words.

Thank You for meeting with Your people and shaping us by Your Word.

Amen.

Key Takeaway

True worship is a whole-life response to God, guided by Scripture. It is marked by reverence, gratitude, repentance, and obedience.

BOOK TWO

UNDERSTAND WHAT IT MEANS TO BE HUMAN

To understand yourself and others, you must start where the Bible starts. God made people with purpose, dignity, and responsibility. Even after sin entered the world, human life still matters because it is God's work. This book will help you see what it means to bear God's image, how sin has affected every part of us, and why we still have real worth. Each chapter includes clear teaching and guided exercises that connect Scripture to daily life. The goal is simple: to think rightly about humanity so you can live wisely before God and love people well.

CHAPTER 1

CREATED IN GOD'S IMAGE

The Bible says humans are made in God's image. This is one of the most important truths you can learn about yourself and every other person. It explains why human life has value, why sin is so serious, and why redemption matters.

Genesis 1:27 says God created mankind in His own image, male and female. This verse gives two clear facts. First, our value is not earned. It is given by God. Second, every human being shares this dignity. Image of God is not reserved for the strong, the healthy, the educated, or the successful. It applies to the unborn child, the elderly, the disabled, the poor, the prisoner, and the stranger. It applies to your neighbor and your enemy.

The image of God does not mean we are divine. We are not little gods. We do not share God's power or His authority as Creator. We are still creatures. We need food, rest, and help. We get sick and we die. We can be wrong. We can be foolish. God is not like that. He is perfect. We are not.

So what does it mean to bear God's image?

At a basic level, it means we were made to reflect Him. A mirror does not create light. It reflects light. In a similar way, humans were made to show something true about God in the world God made.

Scripture points to several ways we reflect God.

First, we reflect God through moral awareness. Humans have a sense that some things are right and others are wrong. That sense can be damaged, ignored, or twisted, but it is still there. We are not driven by instinct alone. We can judge our own choices. We can feel guilt. We can confess. We can seek forgiveness. That moral awareness points to a holy and righteous God.

Second, we reflect God through reason and speech. We can think, plan, and learn. We can speak words that carry meaning. James 3:9 says we bless God and then use the same tongue to curse people made in God's likeness. The verse assumes something important: the way we treat people is tied to the fact that they bear God's image. It also shows that our words matter. Speech can build or destroy. God speaks truth. We should aim to do the same.

Third, we reflect God through relationships. God made us for life with others. From the beginning, human life includes family and community. This does not mean every person must marry. It means no one was made to live as an island. We need friendship, counsel, accountability, and care. We also need to learn patience, kindness, and forgiveness. Those are relational virtues.

Fourth, we reflect God through work and stewardship. God entrusted the earth to human care. We are called to cultivate, protect, and use creation wisely. Work is not a curse by itself. Work existed before sin entered the world. Work became painful after sin, but work itself is still part of God's design. When we do honest work with skill and integrity, we show something of God's order and goodness.

Fifth, we reflect God through creativity. Humans make songs, stories, tools, homes, gardens, and systems. We do not create from nothing like God does. But we do create within what He made. This is one reason art can be beautiful and also why it can be misused. Creativity can be used to serve others or to feed pride.

The image of God also explains why violence and abuse are evil. Genesis 9:6 ties the seriousness of murder to the image of God. Taking a human life is not only harming a body. It is attacking a person who bears God's mark. The same logic applies to cruelty, racism, exploitation, and hatred. These sins treat image-bearers like objects.

At the same time, Scripture is honest about what sin has done to us. The image of God in humans has been damaged by the fall, but it has not been erased. People still have dignity, but we do not reflect God perfectly. Our minds can become dark. Our desires can become disordered. Our relationships can become selfish. Our work can become greedy. We can use our gifts to harm instead of help.

This is why we must be careful with two mistakes.

One mistake is to deny human worth because of sin. Some people look at the brokenness of the world and decide humans are worthless. That is not biblical. People are fallen, but still valuable.

The other mistake is to praise human goodness in a way that ignores sin. Some people speak as if humans are naturally fine and just need better education or better systems. Scripture does not allow that either. Sin is real and deep. We need more than improvement. We need rescue.

So how does the image of God connect to Christ?

Colossians 3:10 says believers put on the new self, which is being renewed in knowledge after the image of its Creator. This is hope. God does not only forgive. He also restores. In Christ, God is repairing what sin has damaged. This renewal is real, but it is also a process. It grows over time as believers learn truth, repent of sin, and walk in obedience.

Ephesians 4:24 speaks of the new self, created after the likeness of God in true righteousness and holiness. This tells us what restoration looks like. God is forming His people to reflect His character again. He shapes how we think, what we love, and how we live.

This chapter gives you a starting point for the rest of this book. If you want to understand humanity, start here: every person is made by God, marked by God, and meant to reflect God. That truth should shape how you view yourself. It should also shape how you treat others, even when they are difficult, even when they sin, even when they disagree with you.

Workbook Section

1) Scripture Reading and Notes

Read each passage. Write one short observation from each. Keep it concrete.

1. Genesis 1:27 (NSV)

    ----

2. Psalm 8:4–6 (NSV)

    ----

3. Genesis 9:6 (NSV)

____

____

4. James 3:9 (NSV)

____

____

5. Colossians 3:10 (NSV)

____

____

6. Ephesians 4:24 (NSV)

____

____

2) Define It in Your Own Words

Write a simple definition.

The image of God means:

____

____

____

____

____

Now write one sentence that says what it does not mean.

____

____

____

____

The image of God does not mean:

____

_____Genesis 9:6 (NSV)______________________

____

____

3) Self-View Check

Answer with honesty. Use full sentences.

1. When do you most forget your God-given value?

    ____

    ____

    ____

    ____

2. What do you usually base your value on instead?
    Examples: approval, success, appearance, performance, control.

    ____

    ____

    ____

    ____

3. How does Genesis 1:27 correct that pattern?

    ____

    ____

    ____

    ____

4) Neighbor-View Check

Pick one person you find hard to love. Do not write their name if you do not want to.

This person is hard for me because:

____

____

____

____

Now connect the truth.

____

____

____

____

Because this person bears God's image, I should treat them by:

Write one specific action you will take this week that shows respect and restraint.

My action step:

----

5) Words and the Image of God

James 3:9 connects the tongue to the image of God.

List three kinds of speech that dishonor image-bearers.

1. ____

2. ____

3. ____

List three kinds of speech that honor image-bearers.

1. ____

2. ____

3. ____

Now write one sentence you need to stop saying, or stop implying, about yourself or others.

Sentence to put away:

Write one sentence you will practice instead.

Sentence to practice:

----

6) Work and Stewardship

Write answers that fit your real life.

1. What is one part of your work or daily responsibility that feels small?

    ----

2. How could you do that task in a way that reflects God's order and care?

    ----

3. What is one resource God has placed in your hands that you can steward better?

    Examples: time, money, attention, health, skills.

    ----

7) Renewal Plan

Colossians 3:10 speaks of renewal. Choose one area where you want God to restore your reflection of Him.

Area for renewal:

Write one habit that supports that renewal.

Habit to begin:

Write one habit that fights against it.

Habit to remove:

Write a short prayer in your own words. If you need a start, use these lines and complete them.

Father, You made me in Your image.

Forgive me for treating myself or others like ____________________ .

Help me reflect You today through my words, choices, and work.

Renew me in true righteousness and holiness.

Amen.

Every person is made in God's image. Sin damages us, but it does not erase our worth. In Christ, God restores His people so they reflect Him with growing truth and love.

CHAPTER 2

HUMAN PURPOSE AND GOD'S DESIGN

People often ask why they are here. Some ask it in quiet moments. Others feel it through stress, boredom, or regret. The Bible does not leave us guessing. God made people with purpose, and His design is good. Purpose is not something we invent. It is something we receive from the One who made us.

From the beginning, God created humans to live under His authority and enjoy His care. Genesis 2:15 says the Lord God placed the man in the garden "to work it and keep it" (NSV). This shows that purpose includes responsibility. God made us to build, tend, guard, and serve. Work is part of God's good plan. It existed before sin entered the world. That means work is not a punishment. It is a gift that gives structure and meaning to life.

Work does not only mean a job. Work includes caring for children, cleaning a home, studying, farming, leading, crafting, and serving neighbors. It includes tasks people notice and tasks nobody sees. God values faithfulness in both. The size of the task does not determine its worth. What matters is how we do it and why we do it.

God's design also includes rest. Humans are not machines. We have limits because we are creatures. God alone has no limits. The pattern of work and rest teaches us humility. It reminds us that the world does not depend on us. Rest is not laziness. It is a way of trusting God. When we rest, we admit we are not in control.

God also designed humans for relationships. Genesis 2:18 says, "It is not good that the man should be alone" (NSV). God made people to live in community. We need others to help us, correct us, encourage us, and share life with us. This does not mean every person must marry. It means no person is meant to live cut off from meaningful relationships.

Human purpose includes family life, friendship, and life among God's people. Relationships are part of how we reflect God's care. In healthy relationships, people practice love, patience, truth, and forgiveness. This is part of God's design for human life.

Most of all, God designed humans to know Him and honor Him. Ecclesiastes 12:13 says, "Fear God and keep his commandments" (NSV). To fear God means to treat Him as God. It means we honor His Word and submit to His will. This is the center of human purpose. Work and relationships matter, but they are not the highest goal. They are meant to be lived under God.

The Bible also teaches stewardship. Stewardship means managing what belongs to someone else. God owns all things. He gives people time, skills, money, opportunities, and responsibilities. We will answer to Him for how we use what He gives. This truth shapes daily life. It shapes how we spend time. It shapes how we treat our bodies. It shapes how we handle money. It shapes how we use words.

Sin has twisted human purpose. Many people live as if they belong to themselves. They chase pleasure, power, approval, or comfort as if those things can carry the weight of meaning. But these things cannot hold the human heart. They may satisfy for a moment, then they fade. This is why people can have full schedules and still feel empty.

God's design offers a better way. The greatest commands are to love God and love neighbor (Mark 12:30–31, NSV). This gives purpose in two directions. Love toward God means worship, trust, obedience, gratitude, and prayer. Love toward neighbor means seeking another person's good with truth and kindness. This kind of love does not depend on mood. It is a choice rooted in God's Word.

When you understand human purpose, you gain clarity. You stop trying to build identity from performance. You stop chasing meaning in things that cannot save. You begin to live with steady direction. You work with integrity. You rest with trust. You pursue relationships with patience. You worship God with reverence. You steward your life as a gift.

God's design does not remove hardship. But it gives a path that makes sense. It gives a reason to keep going. It gives a foundation that does not shift with feelings or trends. You were made by God, for God, and under God. That truth is not a cage. It is freedom.

1) Scripture Reading and Notes

Read each passage. Write one clear observation from each.

1. Genesis 2:15 (NSV)

    ----

2. Genesis 2:18 (NSV)

    ----

3. Ecclesiastes 12:13 (NSV)

    ----

4. Mark 12:30–31 (NSV)

    ----

5. Colossians 3:23 (NSV)

    ----

6. Psalm 90:12 (NSV)

    ----

2) Purpose in Plain Words

Finish the sentence using simple language.

God made me to:

Now write one sentence that describes a purpose you have chased that did not satisfy.

I have chased:

----

3) Work as Part of God's Design

Answer with honesty.

1. What kind of work fills most of your week right now?

   ----

2. What part of your work feels most draining?

   ----

3. What would it look like to do that part "as for the Lord" this week?

   ----

4. What is one attitude you need to repent of in your work?

   Examples: complaining, laziness, harshness, pride, cutting corners.

   ----

4) Rest and Limits

Write answers that match your real life.

1. Where do you ignore your limits?

   ----

2. What is one sign you are running on empty?

   ----

3. What is one boundary you can set this week to protect time with God and healthy rest?

   ----

5) Relationships in God's Design

1. Name one relationship you want to strengthen.

   ----

2. What is one step you can take this week to strengthen it?

   ----

3. What is one habit that harms your relationships?
   Examples: interrupting, sarcasm, cold silence, gossip, anger.

   ----

4. What is one habit you want to replace it with?

   ----

6) Stewardship Check

Write short answers.

1. One gift God has given me is:

   ----

2. One resource God has placed in my care is:

   ----

3. One area where I often waste what God gives is:

Now write one action step you will take in the next 48 hours.

My action step:

----

7) Love God and Love Neighbor

Use Mark 12:30–31.

1. One way I will love God this week is:

    ----

2. One way I will love my neighbor this week is:

    ----

3. One barrier that gets in the way is:

    ----

4. One change I will make is:

Write a short prayer of direction. If you need help, begin here and finish it.

Father, You made me for Your purpose.

Forgive me for chasing meaning in __________________________ .

Help me honor You in my work, my rest, and my relationships.

Teach me to fear You and keep Your commandments with a willing heart.

Amen.

Human purpose is received, not invented. God designed people to worship Him, steward what He gives, and love others with faithful action.

CHAPTER 3

THE FALL: WHAT BROKE IN US

The Bible teaches that God made the world good. He made humans good. But something happened that changed everything. Scripture calls it "the fall." The fall is not a small mistake. It is the entry of sin into human life and into the human heart. It explains why the world is so beautiful and so broken at the same time.

Genesis 3 tells the account. God gave Adam and Eve a clear command. They were free to enjoy God's gifts, but they were not free to define good and evil for themselves. The serpent tempted Eve by questioning God's Word and God's goodness. The temptation was not only about fruit. It was about authority. Would they trust God's command, or would they make themselves the final judge?

They chose rebellion. Eve took and ate. Adam ate too. At that moment, sin entered human life. Their relationship with God changed. Their relationship with each other changed. Their relationship with creation changed. The fall broke what was whole.

The first thing that broke was trust. Sin is not just breaking rules. It is distrusting God's character. It is believing that God is holding back something good. That lie still drives many sins today. People sin because they believe God's way will not satisfy them. They think they must take what they want, their way, in their time.

The second thing that broke was innocence. After they sinned, Adam and Eve felt shame. Genesis 3 says they knew they were naked and they hid. This is important. Before sin, they had nothing to hide. After sin, they felt exposed. Shame entered the human story. Shame is the sense of being unclean, not just guilty. It pushes people to cover up and to pretend.

The third thing that broke was openness with God. Adam and Eve hid from the Lord. They feared His presence. That is what sin does. It makes people run from the One they need most. Instead of confession, they chose hiding. Instead of trust, they chose fear.

The fourth thing that broke was human relationships. When God confronted Adam, Adam blamed Eve. Eve blamed the serpent. Sin produces excuses. It trains the heart to protect itself. It also produces conflict. Genesis 3 shows that harmony was replaced by tension, mistrust, and selfishness.

The fifth thing that broke was creation itself. God pronounced judgment, and the ground was cursed. Work became painful. Life became marked by toil, thorns, and frustration. Pain in childbirth and hardship in labor became part of human life. Death also entered the world. God had warned that the wages of sin would be death. The fall brought separation, decay, and loss.

The fall also explains the spread of sin. Adam was the head of the human race. When he sinned, sin did not stay with him alone. Romans 5:12 teaches that sin came into the world through one man, and death through sin, and so death spread to all people (NSV). This is why every person is born with a sinful nature. We do not become sinners only by copying others. We sin because we are sinners by nature. We inherit a heart bent away from God.

This is hard truth, but it is also honest truth. Many people want to believe humans are basically good and just need better teaching. But Scripture says the problem goes deeper. The heart is corrupted. The will is twisted. Desires are disordered. This is why rules alone cannot fix us. Better habits alone cannot rescue us. We need a new heart.

At the same time, the fall does not erase the image of God. Humans still have dignity. We still have moral awareness. We can still do acts of kindness. But even our "good" acts can be mixed with pride or selfish motives. The fall touched every part of us. It did not destroy us completely, but it damaged us deeply.

Genesis 3 also gives a small beam of hope. God did not destroy Adam and Eve on the spot. He pursued them. He spoke to them. He covered them. And He promised that a descendant would come who would crush the serpent (Genesis 3:15). This is the first promise of a Savior. It shows that God's response to human sin included judgment, but also mercy and a plan of rescue.

Understanding the fall helps you understand yourself. It explains why you struggle with sin even when you know better. It explains why relationships are hard. It explains why work can feel heavy. It explains why suffering exists. It also helps you stop being surprised by human evil. You still grieve it, but you understand its root.

Most of all, the fall prepares you to understand salvation. If the problem is only surface-level, then salvation would only be self-improvement. But if the problem is heart-level, then salvation must be deeper. God must forgive sin and also restore what broke inside us. That is what He does through Christ.

Workbook Section

1) Scripture Reading and Notes

Read each passage. Write one clear observation.

1. Genesis 3:1–7 (NSV)

   ____

   ____

2. Genesis 3:8–13 (NSV)

   ____

   ____

3. Genesis 3:16–19 (NSV)

   ____

   ____

4. Romans 5:12 (NSV)

   ____

   ____

5. James 1:14–15 (NSV)

   ____

   ____

6. Genesis 3:15 (NSV)

   ____

   ____

2) What Broke First?

In Genesis 3, several things break. Write short answers.

1. What lie does the serpent use to tempt?

    ----

2. What emotion shows up right after sin?

    ----

3. What is the first thing Adam and Eve do when they hear God?

    ----

4. How do they respond when confronted?

    ----

3) Trace a Pattern

James 1:14–15 describes how sin grows. Think of a recent temptation you faced. Do not write details that feel unsafe to share. Keep it general.

1. The desire or pull I felt was:

    ----

2. The lie I was tempted to believe was:

    ----

3. The choice I made, or almost made, was:

----

4. The result in my thoughts or relationships was:

Now write one sentence about what you would do differently next time.

Next time I will:

----

4) Shame and Hiding

Answer honestly.

1. What do you tend to hide when you feel shame?
    Examples: feelings, failures, anger, fear, habits.

----

2. What does hiding do to your relationship with God?

----

3. What does hiding do to your relationships with others?

----

4. What is one step of honesty you can take this week?

----

5) The Spread of Sin

Romans 5:12 shows sin spread to all.

1. How does this truth help you understand the world's brokenness?

----

2. How does it help you understand your own struggles?

----

3. What is the danger of blaming only "society" for sin?

----

6) Hope in the Middle of Judgment

Genesis 3:15 is a promise of rescue.

1. What does it tell you about God's response to sin?

----

2. What does it tell you about God's plan?

----

3. How does this give you hope today?

Write a prayer of confession and hope. If you need help, begin here and finish it.

Lord, You made the world good, but sin has broken us.

I confess that I have believed lies about Your Word and Your goodness.

Forgive me for ____.

Help me stop hiding and walk in the light.

Thank You that You promised a Savior and that Your mercy is real.

Amen.

The fall explains what broke in us. Sin damaged our trust, brought shame, fractured relationships, and brought death into the human story. Yet God pursued sinners and promised rescue.

CHAPTER 4

HOW SIN AFFECTS OUR THINKING AND DESIRES

Teaching Section

Sin does more than break rules. Sin bends the inside of a person. It twists how we think and what we want. This is why sin can feel normal, even when it is deadly. It is also why people can know the truth and still choose lies.

Jeremiah 17:9 says the heart is deceitful above all things and sick. That does not mean every thought you have is false. It means your inner life is not a safe guide by itself. Your heart can excuse sin. Your mind can rewrite wrong as right. Your desires can push you toward what harms you.

Sin affects our thinking in several ways.

First, sin darkens the mind. It makes spiritual truth seem foolish. 2 Corinthians 4:4 says the god of this world has blinded the minds of unbelievers. A blind mind cannot see the beauty of Christ. It cannot see sin as sin. It cannot see God as good. This blindness does not mean people lack intelligence. It means the deepest problem is spiritual, not academic.

Second, sin trains us to suppress truth. People can push truth down so they do not have to obey it. They may avoid Scripture. They may avoid godly counsel. They may stay busy so they do not have to think. Over time, the conscience can grow dull. A dull conscience feels less. It warns less. It stops sounding the alarm.

Third, sin distorts our view of God. Many sins begin with a false picture of God. Some think God is distant, so prayer feels useless. Some think God is harsh, so they hide. Some think God is weak, so they take control. But wrong thoughts about God lead to wrong choices. What you believe about God shapes what you do when you are tempted.

Sin also affects our desires.

Desires are not evil by themselves. Hunger is a desire. Rest is a desire. Friendship is a desire. The problem is that sin disorders desire. It takes good things and makes them ruling things. It takes a gift and turns it into a god. It makes the heart say, "I must have this," even when God says no.

James 4:1 says conflicts come from passions at war within us. That verse ties outward trouble to inward desire. When desires rule, people will lie, lash out, and manipulate. They will also envy and resent. They will demand their way. This is not just a personality issue. It is a heart issue.

Sin also makes desire loud. It makes it feel urgent. It tells you, "Do it now," and "You deserve it." Proverbs 14:12 says there is a way that seems right to a man, but its end is the way to death. Temptation often looks right at first. It looks fair. It looks harmless. But it leads to damage.

Here is another way sin harms desire. It teaches us to love the wrong things. Titus 3:3 says people were once foolish, disobedient, led astray, slaves to various passions and pleasures. That word slaves matters. A slave does not feel free. A slave serves a master. Sin makes passions act like a master. It commands. It promises comfort. Then it takes more than it gives.

This is why "follow your heart" is poor advice. Your heart needs guidance. Your heart needs correction. Your heart needs renewal. Proverbs 4:23 says to guard your heart, for from it flow the springs of life. If the spring is polluted, the stream will be polluted too.

So what is the answer?

The Bible does not tell you to trust your thoughts and feelings. It tells you to test them. It tells you to listen to God's Word. It tells you to seek wisdom. It tells you to walk by the Spirit so you do not carry out sinful desires. Galatians 5:16 says, "Walk by the Spirit, and you will not gratify the desires of the flesh" (NSV). This is hope. You are not trapped. God gives help that is stronger than temptation.

Galatians 5:17 explains that the flesh desires what is against the Spirit, and the Spirit desires what is against the flesh. That means there is a real fight inside believers. If you feel that fight, it does not prove you are lost. It may show you are alive. A dead heart does not fight sin. A living heart does.

Sin affects thinking and desire, but God can renew both. Colossians 1:21 says people were once alienated and hostile in mind, doing evil deeds. Then the passage moves toward reconciliation through Christ. God changes the mind and the heart. He does not only forgive the past. He reshapes the present.

How does God reshape us?

First, He gives truth. Truth exposes lies. Psalm 119:105 says God's word is a lamp to your feet and a light to your path. When truth shines, temptation loses some of its pull. You can see the end of the road, not just the first step.

Second, God calls us to repentance. Repentance is a change of mind that leads to a change of direction. It is not self-hate. It is turning from sin because you trust God is better.

Third, God trains desire. This takes time. You may still feel wrong cravings. But you can learn to say no. You can learn to replace lies with truth. You can learn to seek what pleases God. Philippians 2:13 says God works in you, both to will and to work for His good pleasure. God does not only command. He also gives strength.

Fourth, God uses practices that reshape the heart. Scripture reading, prayer, confession, fellowship, and wise boundaries all matter. They are not ways to earn God's love. They are ways to walk in God's help.

This chapter matters because you cannot fight what you do not name. If you think sin is only "bad behavior," you will focus on image. You will try to look good. But if you see sin as an inner problem, you will seek inner change. You will ask God to renew your mind and reorder your desires.

Here is the steady truth to hold. Sin bends what you think and want. God can straighten what sin has bent. He does it through His Word, His Spirit, and a life of humble obedience.

1) Scripture Reading and Notes

Read each passage. Write one clear observation from each.

1. Jeremiah 17:9 (NSV)

   ----

2. 2 Corinthians 4:4 (NSV)

   ----

3. James 4:1 (NSV)

   ----

4. Proverbs 14:12 (NSV)

   ----

5. Proverbs 4:23 (NSV)

   ----

6. Galatians 5:16–17 (NSV)

   ----

7. Philippians 2:13 (NSV)

   ----

2) Spot the Lie, Speak the Truth

Write one lie that temptation often whispers to you. Keep it short.

The lie: ____

Now write a true statement from what you learned in this chapter.

The truth: ______________________________________

Write one sentence you can say in the moment of temptation.

My sentence:

----

3) Map Your Pattern

Think of a recent moment when you felt pulled toward sin. Do not include details you do not want to write down.

1. What was happening right before the temptation?

    ----

2. What did you want in that moment?

    Examples: comfort, control, approval, escape, pleasure.

    ----

3. What did you tell yourself to make it feel okay?

    ----

4. What was the result in your heart or relationships?

Now write one small change you can make next time.

My change:

----

4) Guard the Springs

Proverbs 4:23 says to guard your heart.

List three inputs that shape your thinking each week.

Examples: music, videos, friends, news, social media, books.

1.____

2.____

3.____

Now answer:

1. Which input helps you love what is good?

    ____

    ____

    ____

2. Which input stirs wrong desires?

    ____

    ____

    ____

3. What boundary will you set this week?

    ____

    ____

    ____

My boundary:

    ____

    ____

    ____

5) Walk by the Spirit Plan

Galatians 5:16 calls you to walk by the Spirit. Write a simple plan you can do.

1. One time each day I will open God's Word:

    ____

    ____

    ____

2. One short prayer I will repeat when tempted:

----

3. One person I can ask for prayer or support:

----

4. One wise step I will take to avoid a common trap:

----

6) Desire Check

Write short answers.

1. A good desire I have is:

----

2. A desire that often tries to rule me is:

----

3. One way that ruling desire has harmed me is:

----

4. One better desire I want God to grow in me is:

Write a prayer for a renewed mind and reordered desires. If you need help, begin here and finish it.

Father, my heart can mislead me.

____

____

Shine Your truth on my thoughts.

____

____

Help me guard what I take in.

____

____

Teach me to walk by Your Spirit when I am tempted.

____

____

Change what I want so I want what pleases You.

____

____

Amen.

Key Takeaway

Sin bends our thinking and disorders our desires. God gives truth and strength so we can see clearly, choose wisely, and grow in new wants.

CHAPTER 5

HUMAN WORTH AND DIGNITY AFTER THE FALL

After sin entered the world, something stayed true. People are still made by God, and people still matter. The fall damaged the human heart, but it did not erase human worth. This matters because the world often measures value the wrong way. It measures value by strength, beauty, health, money, influence, or usefulness. God does not measure people that way.

Human dignity rests on God's decision to create humans and to set His mark on them. Even in a broken world, God treats human life as weighty. Proverbs 22:2 says, "The rich and the poor meet together; the Lord is the Maker of them all" (NSV). That verse places rich and poor on the same ground. Both are made by God. Both answer to God. Both have worth that money cannot raise or lower.

This truth protects people who are easily pushed aside. It protects the poor, the unborn, the sick, the elderly, the disabled, the refugee, and the forgotten. It also corrects pride in those who feel secure. If you have wealth, health, or status, those gifts do not make you more human than others. If you lack those things, that lack does not make you less human than others.

Human dignity also reshapes how we treat people we dislike. It is easy to respect those who agree with you. It is harder to respect those who offend you or oppose you. But Scripture calls us to treat people with care because they are God's creatures, even when they are wrong, even when they are difficult. This does not mean we excuse sin. It means we refuse to treat people as trash.

The fall did not erase human value, but it did affect how we see ourselves and others. One of the first fruits of sin is shame. Shame makes a person feel dirty, unwanted, or beyond help. Shame whispers, "You are what you did," or "You are what happened to you." But Scripture separates a person's worth from their worst moment. God's Word is honest about sin, yet it still speaks of human dignity.

Psalm 139:14 says, "I praise you, for I am fearfully and wonderfully made" (NSV). This does not mean every person feels wonderful. It means God's workmanship is real. Your life is not random. Your body and your days are known to God. This truth does not remove pain, but it gives a stable base for identity.

Human dignity also shapes how we view justice. In Job 31:15, Job asks, "Did not he who made me in the womb make him?" (NSV). Job uses creation to argue for fair treatment. He is saying, "God made both of us, so I must not crush another person." That is a strong moral line. The worth of a person is not decided by power. It is decided by God.

In Acts 17:26, Scripture says God "made from one man every nation of mankind" (NSV). This truth confronts racial pride and ethnic hatred. It tells us that humans share a common origin. Differences in culture, language, and appearance do not change shared dignity. Racism is not only a social problem. It is a sin against the God who made people.

Human dignity after the fall also changes how we view suffering. Some people assume suffering means God has rejected them. Others assume suffering means they are worthless. Scripture does not teach that. Many faithful people suffered deeply. Suffering can come through living in a fallen world, through the sin of others, through our own sinful choices, or through trials God uses to shape us. But suffering does not cancel dignity. A wounded person is still a person. A struggling person is still valuable.

This also matters for how we speak. Words can cut a person down to size. They can label someone as hopeless. They can reduce a person to a failure, an addiction, or a diagnosis. But God does not speak that way. He speaks truth, yet He also speaks with purpose. He calls sinners to repent, and He also offers mercy to the humble.

Still, we need balance. Saying every person has dignity does not mean every choice is good. The Bible can affirm human worth while also calling sin sin. A person is valuable even when their behavior is evil. If we forget this, we will either become harsh and cruel, or we will become soft and approving. Scripture calls us to a better path: compassion without compromise.

A clear example is how Jesus treated people who were ignored or despised. He did not treat them like props. He listened. He spoke truth. He showed mercy. He also called people to change. Luke 19:10 says the Son of Man came to seek and to save the lost (NSV). That line holds both truths. People are lost, and people are worth seeking.

This is also where Christian hope becomes practical. If God values people, then Christians must value people. That includes protecting life, speaking with care, and refusing to use others for personal gain. It also includes doing good to those who cannot pay you back, and treating the weak as neighbors, not burdens.

Human dignity after the fall also speaks to your view of yourself. Many people swing between pride and despair. Pride says, "I am above others." Despair says, "I am beyond help." Both forget God. A biblical view says, "I am a creature made by God. I am fallen and I need mercy. Yet I have real worth because God made me and God calls me to Himself."

So what do you do with shame and self-hate? You bring them into the light of truth. You name sin where it exists. You do not excuse it. But you also refuse to let sin define your whole identity. In Christ, God forgives and restores. He calls you His own. That does not erase consequences, but it does change your standing before Him.

Human worth also shapes how you handle conflict. If the person in front of you has dignity, you must speak with restraint. You can disagree without contempt. You can correct without cruelty. You can set boundaries without hatred. You can pursue justice without dehumanizing the wrongdoer.

This chapter is meant to steady you. The fall explains why we are broken. But dignity explains why humans are still precious and why love and justice still matter. If you hold both truths together, you can see people clearly. You will not flatter humanity as if sin is small. You also will not crush humanity as if grace is impossible. You will treat people as God's creatures who need truth, mercy, and hope.

1) Scripture Reading and Notes

Read each passage. Write in your journal one observation from each.

1. Proverbs 22:2 (NSV)

    ----

2. Psalm 139:13–16 (NSV)

    ----

3. Job 31:15 (NSV)

    ----

4. Acts 17:26 (NSV)

    ----

5. Luke 19:10 (NSV)

    ----

6. Matthew 25:40 (NSV)

    ----

2) Define Dignity

Write in your journal a simple definition in your own words.

Human dignity means:

Now write one sentence about what dignity does not depend on.

Human dignity does not depend on:

----

3) Identify False Measures of Worth

Circle or copy any that you struggle with. Then answer the questions.

Common false measures: money, success, grades, appearance, strength, health, marriage, children, popularity, productivity.

1. Which false measure pulls you the most?

   ----

2. When did you start believing that measure mattered most?

   ----

3. What truth from today's passages corrects it?

   ----

4) How You Treat Others

Think of one person you tend to dismiss, ignore, or speak about harshly.

1. What makes it hard for you to honor them?

   ----

2. What does Matthew 25:40 teach you about how God views "the least"?

---

3. What is one respectful action you will take this week?

---

5) Dignity and Conflict

Write short answers.

1. When you disagree with someone, what words do you often want to use?

---

2. What would it look like to correct without contempt?

---

3. Write one sentence you can use in conflict that shows both truth and respect.

---

6) Shame Check

Answer honestly.

1. What is one shame message you hear in your mind?

---

2. Is that message true, partly true, or false? Explain in one or two sentences.

----

3. Replace the shame message with a truth statement from Psalm 139 or Luke 19:10.

----

7) Practice Seeing People Clearly

Choose one group that often gets overlooked in your life or community.

Group:

Write one way you can show practical care in the next seven days.

My plan:

Prayer Response

Write a short prayer. If you need help, begin here and finish it.

Father, You are the Maker of every person.

Forgive me for measuring worth by _______________________ .

Help me treat others with honor, even when it is hard.

Free me from shame that is not from You.

Teach me to see people as You see them.

Amen.

Key Takeaway

The fall damaged humanity, but it did not erase human worth. Every person still has dignity because God made them. This truth shapes how you view yourself and how you treat others.

CHAPTER 6

LIVING AS GOD'S IMAGE BEARERS TODAY

The Bible's teaching about humanity is not meant to stay on paper. It is meant to shape daily life. If people are made in God's image, then life has direction. It also has boundaries. Being an image bearer is both a gift and a calling. It means you belong to God. It means your life is meant to reflect Him in the world.

Living as God's image bearer today begins with identity. Many people try to build identity from achievement, approval, comfort, or control. But these things are unstable. They can be taken away. They also can become idols that rule the heart. A stable identity comes from the Creator. You are a creature made by God, not a self-made project. This truth brings humility and peace at the same time.

It also brings responsibility. Image bearers represent God's character in how they live. This does not mean you will reflect God perfectly. Sin still clings. But it does mean you should seek to reflect God truly. Scripture calls believers to grow in holiness and truth because they belong to the Holy God.

One key area is how you use words. Words reveal the heart. Proverbs 18:21 says death and life are in the power of the tongue (NSV). Image-bearing speech is honest, restrained, and aimed at the good of others. It refuses gossip. It refuses cruel humor. It refuses the half-truth meant to protect yourself. It also refuses flattery that hides fear. Instead, it speaks truth with care.

Another key area is how you treat people. Since every person is made by God, you do not have permission to treat anyone as less than human. This includes people you disagree with. It includes people who have harmed you. It includes people who cannot help you. Living as an image bearer means you practice respect, patience, and justice. You do not excuse sin, but you refuse to dehumanize sinners.

This is also where love becomes practical. 1 John 4:20 says if someone claims to love God but hates his brother, he is a liar (NSV). That is strong language. It shows that love for God is tested by how we treat people. Love is not just a warm feeling. It is a pattern of choices that seek another person's good.

Living as God's image bearer today also shapes how you handle your body. Your body is not a toy and not a god. It is a gift. It is also a trust. What you do with your body matters. This includes sexuality, health, rest, and self-control. Many people treat the body as if it belongs to them alone. Scripture teaches you belong to God. That truth leads to wise boundaries and pure living.

Your work also matters. Work is one way image bearers reflect God's order and care. Whether your work is paid or unpaid, it is part of your calling. Honest work is a form of love. It provides. It serves. It builds. It blesses others. It also trains integrity. Even small tasks can be done with faithfulness.

Living as God's image bearer today also means practicing stewardship. God gives resources, then calls you to use them with wisdom. That includes time, money, attention, and energy. Many people waste life by drifting from one distraction to the next. Wisdom says, "My life is not my own. God gave me days, so I will use them well."

This is also how image bearers respond to culture. Some people blend in and let culture shape them. Others fight culture with anger and pride. But Scripture calls believers to be distinct with humility. Living as an image bearer means you test what you hear and see. You do not accept every message. You also do not become bitter and harsh. You stay grounded in truth, and you practice love.

This includes how you use technology. Technology is a tool. It can help you learn, work, connect, and serve. It can also steal attention, feed lust, stir anger, and build envy. An image bearer should not be ruled by a screen. Wisdom sets limits and chooses what builds up.

Living as God's image bearer today also includes responding to sin in your own life. You will fail at times. The question is not whether you will ever sin again. The question is what you do when you sin. Image-bearing life includes confession, repentance, and renewal. You do not hide. You do not blame. You bring your sin to God. You seek forgiveness. You make changes. You pursue accountability. This is how growth happens.

One more key part is hope. Many people look at the world and feel hopeless. They see violence, corruption, and division. But Scripture teaches that God is at work and will complete His plan. Your faithfulness matters even when the world feels dark. A faithful life is not wasted. God sees it. God uses it. God rewards it.

So how do you begin?

Start with one area. Choose your words, your habits, your relationships, your time. Ask God to help you live as His image bearer in daily choices. Big change often begins with small obedience done consistently.

Living as God's image bearer today is not about showing off. It is about reflecting God with a steady life. It is about honoring Him in the ordinary. It is about loving people in real ways. It is about standing in truth with humility. It is about walking in repentance and hope.

This chapter closes Book Two with a simple aim. You were made to reflect God. Sin damaged that reflection. In Christ, God renews His people. As you live with faith and obedience, the reflection grows clearer.

Workbook Section

1) Scripture Reading and Notes

Read each passage. Write in your journal one observation.

1. Proverbs 18:21 (NSV)

    ----

2. 1 John 4:20 (NSV)

    ----

3. Micah 6:8 (NSV)

    ----

4. Colossians 3:12–14 (NSV)

----

5. Romans 12:2 (NSV)

----

6. Ephesians 4:29 (NSV)

----

2) Image Bearer Inventory

Rate yourself from 1 to 5.

1 = weak right now, 5 = strong right now.

Words that build others up:	1	2	3	4	5
Patience with difficult people:	1	2	3	4	5
Honesty and integrity:	1	2	3	4	5
Use of time and attention:	1	2	3	4	5
Self-control in habits:	1	2	3	4	5

Now answer:

1. Which area needs the most attention?

----

2. Which area is a strength you should thank God for?

----

3) Words Practice

Use Ephesians 4:29.

1. Write one kind of speech you need to stop.

    Examples: sarcasm, gossip, harshness, exaggeration.

    ----

2. Write one sentence you can use instead that gives grace.

    ----

3. Who is one person you will encourage this week?

    ----

4) People Practice

Choose one difficult relationship.

1. What is one way you have been tempted to treat this person as less than human?

    ----

2. What does 1 John 4:20 call you to do differently?

    ----

3. What is one respectful action you will take in the next seven days?

    ----

5) Culture and Mind Renewal

Romans 12:2 calls believers not to be shaped by the world.

1. What message from culture most pressures you?

    Examples: "You are what you achieve," "Do what feels right," "Get even."

    ----

2. What truth from Scripture replaces it?

    ----

3. What is one boundary you can set to protect your mind this week?

    ----

6) Stewardship Plan

Write short answers.

1. One time-waster I need to reduce is:

    ----

2. One habit that helps me focus on what matters is:

    ----

3. One act of service I will do this week is:

Write a prayer of daily faithfulness. If you need help, begin here and finish it.

Father, You made me to reflect You.

Forgive me for the ways I have failed in my words and choices.

Help me live as Your image bearer today by_______________________ .

Teach me to love others with truth and patience.

Renew my mind and strengthen my self-control.

Amen.

Key Takeaway

Living as God's image bearer today means reflecting God in ordinary life. It shows up in words, relationships, habits, and choices. God helps His people grow in a clearer reflection through truth, repentance, and daily faithfulness.

BOOK THREE
GRASP HOW SALVATION REALLY WORKS

Salvation is not self-help and it is not something we earn. It is God's rescue for sinners through Jesus Christ. This book will help you see the Bible's full picture of salvation, from God's first move toward us to the new life He produces in us. You will study Christ's saving work, what repentance and faith mean, why justification matters, how growth in holiness happens, and how God gives real assurance. Each chapter includes clear teaching and guided questions so you can understand the gospel more clearly and respond with worship, trust, and obedience.

CHAPTER 1

SALVATION BEGINS WITH GOD'S INITIATIVE

Teaching Section

Many people think salvation begins when a person decides to seek God. The Bible shows a deeper truth. Salvation begins with God seeking the sinner. If God did not move first, no one would come. This is not because people lack the ability to read or learn. It is because sin bends the heart away from God.

Ephesians 2:1 says we were dead in trespasses and sins (NSV). Dead people do not rescue themselves. They do not reach for help. They need life given to them. This verse is meant to humble us, not crush us. It tells the truth about our condition so we will see the greatness of grace.

God's initiative shows up in three clear ways: His choice, His call, and His gift of new life.

First, God chooses. Scripture teaches that God's saving plan is not an emergency fix. It is eternal and intentional. 2 Timothy 1:9 says God saved us and called us, not because of our works, but because of His own purpose and grace, given in Christ before time began (NSV). That means grace is not God reacting to you. Grace is God acting from His own will, according to His own plan.

This does not mean humans are robots. People make real choices. People really believe, really repent, and really follow. But behind that response is God's gracious work. Salvation begins with God, not with human effort.

Second, God calls. John 6:44 says no one can come to Christ unless the Father draws him (NSV). That drawing is not a gentle suggestion that can be ignored without consequence. It is God bringing a person to Himself through truth and the Spirit's work. God uses means like preaching, Scripture reading, a conversation, a warning, or a crisis. The outward moment can look ordinary, but God is doing something deeper.

We see a clear example in Acts 16:14. A woman named Lydia listened to Paul, and the text says the Lord opened her heart to pay attention to what was said (NSV). Lydia heard real words. She used her mind. She responded. Yet Scripture gives the credit to God's work in her heart. That is what divine initiative looks like. God makes the message effective.

Third, God gives new life. Ezekiel 36:26 says God gives a new heart and a new spirit (NSV). He does not simply offer advice or moral improvement. He changes what is inside. He takes a heart of stone and gives a heart of flesh. A stone heart is cold and stubborn. A flesh heart is living and responsive. This new heart is what makes repentance real and faith possible.

If salvation begins with God's initiative, then what is our part?

Our part is to respond to God's call with repentance and faith. God does not save people against their will. He changes the will so the person willingly comes to Christ. The sinner who once loved darkness begins to love the light. The person who once resisted truth begins to receive it. This response is real, personal, and necessary. Yet it is also a gift of grace.

Ephesians 2:8–9 says we are saved by grace through faith, and this is not our own doing (NSV). The whole rescue is God's gift. This removes boasting. No one can say, "I saved myself." It also removes despair. If salvation depended on your strength, you would lose it. If it depends on God's mercy, you can rest in His faithfulness.

God's initiative also shows His character. He is not a reluctant Savior. He is not waiting for sinners to prove they are worth saving. Romans 5:8 says God shows His love in that Christ died for us while we were still sinners (NSV). God loved us at our worst, not after we cleaned ourselves up.

This truth also answers a common fear. Some people think, "I want God, but I do not know if He wants me." Scripture answers that fear with clarity. God invites sinners. He commands repentance. He promises mercy to those who come. Jesus says whoever comes to Him, He will never cast out (John 6:37, NSV). God's initiative does not cancel human responsibility. It gives hope that your coming is not pointless.

God's initiative also changes how we talk about salvation. We do not treat salvation as a product for self-improvement. We do not treat it as a reward for good behavior. We treat it as rescue for helpless sinners. We also treat it as adoption into God's family, not a cold legal transaction alone.

It also changes how we pray for others. If salvation depends on God's work, then prayer is not a last resort. Prayer is a natural response. We ask God to open eyes, soften hearts, and give repentance. We speak the gospel, and we also pray that God will make it fruitful.

God's initiative changes how we view our past, too. Many believers look back and see a trail of sin and regret. They think, "How could God ever want me?" But if salvation starts with God's purpose and grace, then your past does not surprise Him. It does not excuse sin, but it does show the depth of mercy. God is not saving the most impressive people. He is saving sinners.

This truth should produce humility. If God moved first, you cannot look down on others. You cannot treat unbelievers as if you are naturally better. You were dead too. You were blind too. God showed mercy. That mercy should make you patient and compassionate with others.

This truth should also produce confidence. If God began the work, He will not abandon it. He does not start what He cannot finish. When doubts come, you can look away from your performance and look to God's promise.

So here is the main point of this chapter: salvation begins with God's initiative. He plans, He calls, and He gives new life. Our response matters, but it rests on His grace. That truth makes worship deeper, prayer stronger, and hope steadier.

Workbook Section

1) Scripture Reading and Notes

Read each passage. Write one clear truth you learn from it.

1. Ephesians 2:1 (NSV)

------- ---

2. 2 Timothy 1:9 (NSV)

3. John 6:44 (NSV)

4. Acts 16:14 (NSV)

5. Ezekiel 36:26 (NSV)

6. Ephesians 2:8–9 (NSV)

7. Romans 5:8 (NSV)

8. John 6:37 (NSV)

2) Put It in Your Own Words

Complete these sentences with simple language.

1. Salvation begins with God because:

2. God's call is needed because:

3. A new heart is needed because:

Now write one sentence that explains how this teaching guards you from pride.

My sentence:

Write one sentence that explains how it guards you from despair.

My sentence:

----

3) Trace Your Story

Think back to how you first began to take God seriously. If you do not know Christ yet, answer using what you have seen or heard in your life.

1. What circumstances brought the gospel close to you?

   Examples: a person, a sermon, a Bible reading, a crisis, a quiet season.

   ----

2. What truth began to press on your heart?

   ----

3. What changed in your desires or thinking over time?

   ----

4. Where do you see God's initiative in your story?

----

4) Check Your Assumptions

Choose the statement that sounds most like you, then write a response based on today's passages.

A. "God helps those who help themselves."

B. "I am too far gone for God to want me."

C. "I found God because I was smarter or more serious."

D. "If God is the one who begins salvation, my choices do not matter."

My statement:

Now correct it using one verse from the list above.

Verse and correction:

----

5) Prayer for Someone Who Does Not Believe

Pick one person you care about. Do not write their name if you prefer privacy.

1. What makes you burdened for this person?

----

2. What is one obstacle you see in their life?

----

3. Based on Acts 16:14 and Ezekiel 36:26, what should you ask God
    to do?

Write a short prayer of intercession:

Father, please work in this person's heart.

Open their mind to Your truth.

Give them a new heart that responds to Christ.

Use Your Word to draw them to Jesus.

Amen.

6) Respond With Gratitude and Obedience

Answer with concrete steps.

1. If salvation is a gift, what is one way you will thank God today?

----

2. What is one habit that helps you stay close to God's Word?

----

3. What is one small act of obedience you will do this week as a response to grace?

Prayer Response

Write a prayer of humility. If you need help, complete these lines.

Lord, I confess that I often want credit for what only You can do.

Thank You for taking the first step toward me.

Thank You for grace that I did not earn.

Help me respond with faith, repentance, and steady obedience.

Amen.

Key Takeaway

Salvation begins with God's initiative. He plans with purpose, calls with power, and gives new life by grace. Our response is real, but it rests on what God has done first.

CHAPTER 2

CHRIST'S WORK SECURES OUR SALVATION

Teaching Section

Salvation is not built on what we do. It is built on what Christ has done. If your peace depends on your performance, you will always feel unsure. But if your peace rests on Christ's finished work, you can stand on firm ground.

The Bible teaches that Jesus did not come only to teach. He came to save. He lived a life of perfect obedience, died a real death in our place, and rose from the dead. His work is complete and effective. It does not need to be improved by human effort. It needs to be received by faith.

To understand Christ's work, we need to see why it was necessary.

God is holy. God is just. Sin is not a small problem. It is rebellion against God. Because God is just, sin must be judged. Because God is merciful, He provides a Savior. The cross is where God's justice and mercy meet.

1 Peter 2:24 says, "He himself bore our sins in his body on the tree" (NSV). That sentence is clear. Christ carried our sins. He bore the weight of guilt and judgment. He did not die as a victim of bad politics only. He died as a substitute. He took what we deserved.

This is often called substitution. Substitution means one person stands in the place of another. If Christ did not stand in our place, we would still stand under God's judgment. But Christ took the penalty so that sinners who trust Him can be forgiven.

Isaiah 53:5 says He was pierced for our transgressions and crushed for our iniquities (NSV). That passage shows the same truth. Christ suffered for sins that were not His. He was not paying for His own guilt. He was paying for ours.

Christ's work also includes His obedient life. Jesus did not only die. He lived in perfect faithfulness. He obeyed the Father in every thought, word, and action. Where Adam failed, Christ obeyed. Romans 5:19 says, "By the one man's obedience the many will be made righteous" (NSV). Christ's obedience counts for those who belong to Him. This is part of what it means to be saved by grace.

Christ's work is also a sacrifice. Ephesians 5:2 says Christ loved us and gave Himself up for us, a fragrant offering to God (NSV). In the Old Testament, sacrifices pointed forward. They showed that sin requires death and that God provides a way for guilt to be covered. Those sacrifices were limited. They were repeated. They could not change the heart. But Christ's sacrifice is final and sufficient.

Hebrews 10:12 says Christ offered one sacrifice for sins forever, then sat down at the right hand of God (NSV). Sitting down shows completion. Priests stood daily because their work was never finished. Christ sat down because His saving work was done.

Christ's work also includes redemption. Redemption means being bought back. Sin enslaves. It binds people through guilt and corrupt desires. Christ paid the price to free His people. Mark 10:45 says the Son of Man came to give His life as a ransom for many (NSV). A ransom is a payment that sets someone free. Christ's blood is that payment.

Christ's work also includes reconciliation. Sin breaks fellowship with God. It creates distance and hostility. But Christ brings peace. Colossians 1:20 says God made peace by the blood of His cross (NSV). Peace with God does not come from trying harder. It comes through Christ removing the barrier of guilt.

Then there is the resurrection. If Jesus stayed dead, we would have no hope. The resurrection is God's public declaration that Christ's sacrifice was accepted. It shows Christ has conquered death. It also guarantees that believers will be raised. 1 Corinthians 15:20 says Christ has been raised as the firstfruits of those who have fallen asleep (NSV). Firstfruits means the first part of a harvest that promises the rest will follow. Christ's resurrection is the promise of our resurrection.

The resurrection also proves Christ is Lord. Romans 1:4 says He was declared to be the Son of God in power by His resurrection (NSV). That does not mean He became God then. It means His identity was shown with power and clarity.

So how does Christ's work secure salvation?

It secures salvation because it deals with the real problem. The real problem is guilt before a holy God. The cross deals with guilt. The real problem is death and separation. The resurrection deals with death. The real problem is bondage to sin. Christ's ransom frees. The real problem is hostility with God. Christ reconciles.

This also means salvation is not fragile. If Christ's work is complete, then the foundation does not shift with your feelings. You can have weak faith and still have a strong Savior. Your faith is not the power. Christ is the power. Faith is the hand that receives Him.

Still, this teaching must be held with care. Some people hear "Christ did it all" and think obedience does not matter. But the Bible never uses grace to excuse sin. It uses grace to change sinners. 1 Peter 2:24 says Christ bore our sins so that we might die to sin and live to righteousness (NSV). Salvation produces a new direction.

Christ's work also leads to worship. When you see the cost of your redemption, pride dies. Gratitude grows. When you see the mercy of God, fear of earning fades. Love and obedience rise.

This chapter is meant to steady your heart. When you feel accused, look to the cross. When you feel hopeless, look to the empty tomb. When you feel trapped, look to the ransom Christ paid. Salvation is secure because Christ's work is secure.

Workbook Section

1) Scripture Reading and Notes

Read each passage. Write one clear truth about Christ's work.

1. 1 Peter 2:24 (NSV)

____

____

2. Isaiah 53:5 (NSV)

____

____

3. Romans 5:19 (NSV)

____

____

4. Ephesians 5:2 (NSV)

---

5. Hebrews 10:12 (NSV)

---

6. Mark 10:45 (NSV)

---

7. Colossians 1:20 (NSV)

---

8. 1 Corinthians 15:20 (NSV)

---

2) Put the Gospel in One Paragraph

Write 4 to 6 sentences that explain what Christ did to save sinners. Keep it simple.

My paragraph:

---

3) Substitution and the Cross

Answer with your own words.

1. What does it mean that Christ "bore our sins"?

---

2. Why is substitution necessary if God is just?

----

3. What happens if you remove substitution from the gospel?

----

4) Finished Work Check

Hebrews 10:12 says Christ sat down after offering one sacrifice.

1. What does "finished" mean in this context?

----

2. Where are you tempted to add your own efforts to Christ's work?

   Examples: trying to earn forgiveness, trying to deserve love, fear-based performance.

----

3. What truth from today's passages corrects that fear?

----

5) The Resurrection and Hope

Answer with short, clear sentences.

1. Why does the resurrection matter for forgiveness?

----

2. What does "firstfruits" tell you about your future?

____

____

3. How should resurrection hope shape the way you face suffering?

____

____

6) Application: From Gratitude to Obedience

Use 1 Peter 2:24.

1. What is one sin pattern you need to "die to"?

____

____

2. What is one righteous habit you want to practice instead?

____

____

3. What is one small step you will take in the next 48 hours?

____

____

Prayer Response

Write a prayer of thanks. If you need help, complete these lines.

Lord Jesus, thank You for bearing my sins.

____

____

Thank You for Your obedience and Your sacrifice.

____

____

Thank You that Your work is complete and enough.

____

____

Help me die to sin and live to righteousness as a response to Your mercy.

____

____

Amen.

Key Takeaway

Christ's obedient life, atoning death, and resurrection secure salvation. His work is complete, and it gives real peace to sinners who trust Him.

CHAPTER 3

FAITH AND REPENTANCE ARE BOTH REQUIRED

The Bible teaches that salvation is a gift of grace, received through faith. It also teaches that a saved person turns from sin. These two responses belong together. Faith and repentance are not competing ideas. They are two sides of one response to the gospel.

Jesus began His public preaching with a clear call: "Repent and believe in the gospel" (Mark 1:15, NSV). Notice the order and the pairing. Repent and believe. Not repent without believing. Not believe without repenting. The gospel calls you to trust Christ and to turn from sin.

Faith means trusting Jesus Christ as Savior and Lord. Faith is not mere agreement with facts. It is personal reliance. It is resting your hope on Christ, not on yourself. Romans 10:9 says if you confess with your mouth that Jesus is Lord and believe in your heart that God raised Him from the dead, you will be saved (NSV). Faith involves the heart and the life. It includes believing and confessing.

Faith also means you stop trying to earn God's acceptance. You stop presenting your record as if it could save you. You come empty-handed. You receive Christ as your only hope. Faith is not a work that earns salvation. Faith is the open hand that receives a gift.

Repentance means turning away from sin and turning to God. It includes a change of mind, a change of direction, and a change in what you love. In Acts 2, Peter preached Christ. The people were cut to the heart and asked what they should do. Peter answered, "Repent and be baptized" (Acts 2:38, NSV). He did not offer them a way to fix themselves. He called them to turn from sin and to come to Christ.

Repentance is often misunderstood. Some people think repentance means paying for sin through shame. Others think repentance means promising God you will never fail again. Scripture presents a better picture. Repentance is honest turning. It is agreeing with God about sin and turning away from it because you trust God's mercy.

2 Corinthians 7:10 says godly grief produces repentance that leads to salvation without regret, while worldly grief produces death (NSV). That verse helps us see the difference between true repentance and mere regret.

Worldly grief is sadness because of consequences. It says, "I got caught," or "I ruined my life," or "I look bad." It may feel intense, but it often stays self-focused. It can lead to despair, bitterness, or more sin.

Godly grief is sorrow that begins with God. It says, "I have sinned against the Lord." It takes responsibility. It does not blame others. It does not excuse. It does not hide behind weak apologies. It turns toward God, trusting His mercy, and it produces change over time.

Repentance also does not mean you clean yourself up before coming to Christ. You repent by coming. You do not fix your heart first, then come. You come with your sin, confess it, and ask God to change you. Repentance is not a price you pay. It is the posture of a person who knows they need grace.

Some people worry that repentance adds works to the gospel. It does not. Repentance does not earn forgiveness. Christ earns forgiveness. Repentance is the right response to forgiveness offered. If someone says they trust Christ but refuses to turn from known sin, their claim is empty. A person cannot cling to rebellion and claim loyalty to Jesus at the same time.

This is why faith and repentance must stay together. Faith without repentance becomes empty words. Repentance without faith becomes self-salvation. Faith says, "Christ is my hope." Repentance says, "Sin is not my master." Both are part of turning to God.

True faith always leads to a changed direction, even if growth is slow. When the heart truly trusts Christ, it begins to hate what God hates and love what God loves. That does not mean instant perfection. It means a new path.

Repentance also continues throughout the Christian life. It is not only the first step. Believers still fight sin. Believers still need confession. Believers still need to turn from wrong desires and wrong habits. The difference is that repentance now happens within a relationship of grace. You do not repent to become God's child. You repent because you are God's child.

Here is a simple way to remember it:

- Faith looks to Christ.
- Repentance turns from sin.
- Both responses happen as you come to God.

This chapter also helps with assurance. Some people look for assurance only in feelings. Feelings rise and fall. Scripture points you to Christ's work and to the fruit of a changed life. If you trust Christ and your life shows a growing pattern of turning from sin, that is evidence of real faith. If you claim faith but love sin without resistance, that should warn you.

At the same time, repentance should not become self-hate. Some people confess sin with no hope. They stay stuck in shame. Godly repentance leads to life. It leads to honesty, humility, and change. It also leads to deeper joy because it brings you back into the light.

A steady gospel response is not complicated. You turn from sin and you trust Christ. You do not save yourself. You come to the One who saves. You do not bargain. You do not pretend. You come with honest confession and true reliance.

So the main point is this: faith and repentance are both required because the gospel is a call to receive Christ and to leave sin. Christ does not only forgive. He also leads. When you come to Him, you come to a Savior and a Lord.

Workbook Section

1) Scripture Reading and Notes

Read each passage. Write one clear truth from each.

1. Mark 1:15 (NSV)

    ----

2. Romans 10:9 (NSV)

    ----

3. Acts 2:37–38 (NSV)

----

4. 2 Corinthians 7:10 (NSV)

----

5. Luke 13:3 (NSV)

----

6. Acts 20:21 (NSV)

----

2) Define the Terms

Write simple definitions in your own words.

Faith is:

Repentance is:

Now write one sentence that explains why they belong together.

They belong together because:

----

3) Worldly Grief or Godly Grief

Use 2 Corinthians 7:10. Think of a time you felt sorry about a wrong choice.

1. What were you most upset about at first?

----

2. Did you focus more on consequences or on sin against God?

----

3. What did your sorrow produce?

    Examples: excuses, hiding, anger, confession, change, seeking help.

----

4. What would godly grief look like in a similar situation next time?

----

4) Faith Check

Romans 10:9 connects belief and confession.

1. Write one sentence that states who Jesus is to you.

----

2. Write one sentence that states what you are trusting Him for.

----

3. Write one sentence that shows what you are no longer trusting for acceptance with God.

    Examples: good works, church attendance, being "better than others."

----

5) Repentance in Real Life

Choose one area where you need to turn from sin. Keep it specific.

1. The sin pattern is:

    ____

2. The common trigger is:

    ____

3. The lie I tend to believe is:

    ____

4. The truth from today's passages that corrects the lie is:

    ____

5. One change I will make this week is:

    ____

6) Two-Part Response Plan

Write a short plan that includes both faith and repentance.

Faith step: One way I will look to Christ daily this week is:

____

____

Repentance step: One way I will turn from sin daily this week is:

____

____

Add one support step.

Support step: One person I can ask to pray for me or check in with me
is:

____

____

7) Confession Practice

Write a short confession that is clear and direct. Avoid vague words
like "mistakes."

I have sinned by:

____

____

I was wrong because:

I ask God to forgive me through Christ because:

I will take this step of change:

Write a short prayer. If you need help, use these lines and complete them.

Lord Jesus, I turn from my sin and I turn to You.

I trust You as my Savior and my Lord.

Forgive me for _________________________________ .

Give me strength to walk in a new direction, starting with ________ .

Thank You for mercy that is real and free.

Amen.

Faith receives Christ. Repentance turns from sin. Both belong together as the gospel response, because Christ saves sinners and leads them into a new way of life.

110

CHAPTER 4

JUSTIFIED BY FAITH ALONE

Many people think salvation means God helps good people become better. The Bible teaches something more shocking and more hopeful. God justifies sinners. To justify means God declares a person righteous in His court. It is a legal verdict. It is not God pretending you never sinned. It is God counting you as righteous because of Jesus Christ.

Romans 3:24 says people are "justified by his grace as a gift, through the redemption that is in Christ Jesus" (NSV). Notice the words grace and gift. Justification is not payment for good behavior. It is God's free act toward those who do not deserve it.

This raises a question. How can a just God declare guilty people righteous? Romans 3:26 answers it by showing what Christ did. God is "just and the justifier of the one who has faith in Jesus" (NSV). God remains just because sin is truly judged. God can justify because Jesus took the penalty and provided perfect righteousness.

Justification is connected to Christ in two ways.

First, Christ's death removes guilt. Romans 4:25 says Jesus was delivered up for our trespasses and raised for our justification (NSV). His death deals with the charge against us. His resurrection confirms the verdict.

Second, Christ's obedience provides righteousness. God does not justify by lowering His standard. His standard is perfect righteousness. The good news is that Christ met that standard. When you trust Him, God counts Christ's righteousness to you. This is why justification brings peace. It does not rest on your best day. It rests on Christ.

Galatians 2:16 says a person is not justified by works of the law but through faith in Jesus Christ (NSV). This verse is direct. Works cannot justify. Law-keeping cannot justify. Even religious effort cannot justify. Faith is the means God uses, because faith looks away from self and toward Christ.

Faith is not a good deed that earns a reward. Faith is reliance. It is resting your hope on Christ alone. Romans 4:5 says God justifies "the one who does not work but believes" (NSV). That verse does not praise laziness. It attacks pride. It says you cannot earn your verdict. You must receive it.

This is why the phrase "faith alone" matters. It does not mean faith is alone in the Christian life. True faith produces obedience over time. But faith alone is the only instrument of justification. Your works are not part of the basis for God's verdict. If they were, you would never have peace.

Justification also differs from sanctification. Justification is God's once-for-all verdict. It does not increase over time. You are either justified or not. Sanctification is the lifelong process of growth in holiness. It does increase over time. Many people confuse these two. When they sin, they think God's verdict has changed. But if you are justified, the verdict is settled.

This does not make sin harmless. Sin still grieves God and damages fellowship and joy. But sin does not overturn justification. A judge does not reverse a lawful verdict every time the adopted child stumbles. In Christ, the verdict stands. That truth helps you repent with hope instead of panic.

Justification also answers the question of boasting. If salvation is partly earned, people will compare themselves. They will feel proud or crushed. Romans 3:27 says boasting is excluded (NSV). Faith shuts the mouth of pride. It leaves room only for gratitude.

Justification also brings peace with God. Romans 5:1 says, "Since we have been justified by faith, we have peace with God through our Lord Jesus Christ" (NSV). Peace is not just a calm feeling. It is a real change in relationship. God is no longer against you as judge. He is for you as Father.

This truth changes how you face accusation. You may be accused by your own conscience. You may be accused by other people. You may even feel spiritual accusation. The answer is not to list your good deeds. The answer is to point to Christ. Your hope is not, "I did better." Your hope is, "Christ is enough."

This truth also changes how you treat others. If you were justified by grace, you cannot treat people with cold pride. You cannot look down on those who struggle. You can speak truth, but with patience. You can correct, but without contempt. You can forgive, because you were forgiven at great cost.

It also changes how you serve. You do not obey to earn God's love. You obey because you already have it in Christ. You serve out of gratitude, not fear. This makes service steadier. It also makes it more joyful.

Philippians 3:9 shows Paul's heart. He wanted to be found in Christ, not having a righteousness of his own, but the righteousness that comes through faith (NSV). That is the goal of every believer. Not self-righteousness, but Christ-righteousness. Not a shaky record, but a solid Savior.

So here is the main point. Justification is God's gracious verdict, given to sinners through faith in Jesus Christ. It is not earned by works. It is not improved by works. It produces peace, humility, and a life of grateful obedience.

Workbook Section

1) Scripture Reading and Notes

Read each passage. Write one clear truth about justification.

1. Romans 3:24 (NSV)

    ____

    ____

2. Romans 3:26 (NSV)

    ____

    ____

3. Galatians 2:16 (NSV)

    ____

    ____

4. Romans 4:5 (NSV)

    ____

    ____

5. Romans 4:25 (NSV)

----

6. Romans 5:1 (NSV)

----

7. Philippians 3:9 (NSV)

----

2) Define the Word

Write a simple definition.

Justification means:

Now write one sentence that explains what justification is not.

Justification is not:

----

3) Two Common Confusions

Answer in short sentences.

1. How is justification different from "God making me a better person"?

----

2. How is justification different from sanctification?

----

3. Why does mixing these up steal peace?

----

4) Replace Self-Talk With Truth

Write one sentence you say to yourself when you feel guilty or afraid.

My guilt sentence:

Now replace it with a truth statement based on Romans 5:1 or Romans 3:24.

My truth statement:

Write one sentence you can say out loud when you feel accused.

My spoken sentence:

----

5) Works and the Heart

Galatians 2:16 says works cannot justify.

1. Where are you tempted to "prove" yourself to God?
   Examples: being perfect, never failing, doing more, being noticed.

   ----

2. What fear is under that impulse?

   ----

3. What truth from today's passages answers that fear?

----

6) Peace With God Practice

Romans 5:1 speaks of peace with God.

1. What do you think God feels toward you on your worst day?

----

2. What does Romans 5:1 say is true if you are justified by faith?

----

3. How should that truth change the way you pray this week?

----

7) Gratitude Response

Write three short lines of gratitude that flow from being justified.

1. Thank You, Lord, for:

----

2. Thank You, Lord, for:

----

3. Thank You, Lord, for:

Now write one act of obedience you will do this week as a response to grace.

My act of obedience:

Write a prayer of trust. If you need help, complete these lines.

Father, thank You for justifying sinners by grace.

I stop trying to earn what Christ has already secured.

When I feel accused, help me rest in Your verdict.

Teach me to obey You out of gratitude, not fear.

Amen.

Justification is God's once-for-all verdict that a sinner is righteous in Christ. It is received by faith, not earned by works, and it brings real peace with God.

CHAPTER 5

SANCTIFIED FOR A NEW WAY OF LIFE

God does not save people only to forgive them. He saves people to change them. This change is called sanctification. Sanctification is the process by which God makes His people more like Christ in real life. It is not instant perfection. It is steady growth. It is learning to put sin to death and to practice obedience from the heart.

1 Thessalonians 4:3 says, "This is the will of God, your sanctification" (NSV). That verse is simple. God's will for His people is not a mystery. He wants you to grow in holiness. Holiness means being set apart for God, living in a way that fits His character.

Sanctification is different from justification. Justification is God's verdict. It happens once. Sanctification is God's work of growth. It continues throughout your life. Justification changes your status. Sanctification changes your conduct. Both are gifts of grace, but they are not the same.

Sanctification begins with union with Christ. If you belong to Christ, you are joined to Him. That union is real. Romans 6:11 tells believers to consider themselves dead to sin and alive to God in Christ Jesus (NSV). That means your relationship to sin has changed. Sin is no longer your master. You still feel temptation. You still can fall. But you do not belong to sin anymore.

Sanctification also involves a real fight. Galatians 5:17 says the flesh desires what is against the Spirit, and the Spirit desires what is against the flesh (NSV). That conflict is part of the Christian life. Some believers feel discouraged by the fight. They think, "If I were really saved, I would not struggle." Scripture says the opposite. The struggle often shows that the Spirit is at work. A heart that is dead in sin does not fight sin. A living heart does.

God sanctifies His people through truth. John 17:17 says, "Sanctify them in the truth; your word is truth" (NSV). God uses Scripture to shape thinking, expose sin, and guide obedience. If you neglect God's Word, you will not grow well. You might still have religious activity, but your inner life will stay weak.

Sanctification also happens through daily choices. Romans 12:2 says believers are transformed by the renewal of the mind (NSV). The mind is renewed when you replace lies with truth, and when you practice thinking God's thoughts. This affects desires and habits over time.

Sanctification includes putting off sin and putting on righteousness. Ephesians 4:22–24 teaches this pattern. Put off the old self, be renewed, and put on the new self (NSV). This helps you think clearly about change. You do not only stop bad habits. You replace them with good habits. If you stop lying, you practice truth. If you stop bitterness, you practice forgiveness. If you stop lust, you pursue purity and wise boundaries. This is a practical pathway for growth.

Sanctification also includes discipline. Discipline is training, not punishment. Hebrews 12:10 says God disciplines us for our good, that we may share His holiness (NSV). God's discipline can include conviction, correction through Scripture, and hard lessons that expose idols. Discipline is proof of God's fatherly care. A loving father trains his children.

This is where many believers need balance. Some people treat sanctification as if it depends mainly on willpower. They try harder, fail, and then feel crushed. Others treat sanctification as if effort does not matter. They say, "God will change me if He wants," and they stay passive. Scripture calls you to active dependence. God works, and you work. Philippians 2:12–13 says work out your salvation with fear and trembling, for God is the one who works in you (NSV). That passage holds both truths. You do not grow without God. You also do not grow without effort.

Sanctification is also shaped by the church. God does not grow His people in isolation. He uses preaching, fellowship, correction, encouragement, and shared worship. Hebrews 10:24–25 calls believers to stir one another up to love and good works and not neglect meeting together (NSV). If you try to live the Christian life alone, you will be more vulnerable to sin and discouragement.

Sanctification also includes suffering. God uses trials to refine faith. James 1:2–4 says trials produce steadfastness, and steadfastness leads toward maturity (NSV). That does not mean suffering is pleasant. It means suffering is not wasted in God's hands. God can use hardship to expose pride, deepen prayer, and strengthen obedience.

Over time, sanctification produces fruit. You may not notice change day to day, but you can often see it over months and years. Growth may look like slower anger, quicker confession, more self-control, more patience, more love for Scripture, and more desire to serve others. Growth also includes learning to hate sin, not only because it has consequences, but because it dishonors God.

Sanctification does not mean you never fail. When you fail, you return to Christ. You confess sin. You ask for help. You make changes. You keep going. Proverbs 24:16 says the righteous falls seven times and rises again (NSV). That verse does not excuse sin. It describes persistence. God's people get up because God gives grace.

Sanctification also protects assurance. Not because your growth earns salvation, but because growth is evidence of life. If a tree is alive, it bears fruit in time. If a believer is alive in Christ, change will show. That change may be slow. It may be uneven. But it will be real.

So here is the main point. Sanctification is God's work of making His people holy in real life. It is a process that includes truth, effort, church life, discipline, and grace. You are not saved by your growth, but you are saved for growth. A new Savior leads to a new way of life.

Workbook Section

1) Scripture Reading and Notes

Read each passage. Write one clear truth about sanctification.

1. 1 Thessalonians 4:3 (NSV)

   ____

   ____

2. John 17:17 (NSV)

   ____

   ____

3. Romans 6:11 (NSV)

----

4. Philippians 2:12–13 (NSV)

----

5. Hebrews 12:10 (NSV)

----

6. Hebrews 10:24–25 (NSV)

----

7. James 1:2–4 (NSV)

----

2) Clarify the Difference

Write short answers.

1. Justification is:

----

2. Sanctification is:

----

3. Why does confusing them hurt your faith?

----

3) Identify One Growth Area

Choose one area where you want to grow. Keep it specific.

My growth area is:

Now answer:

1. What usually triggers this sin or weakness?

    ----

2. What lie do you tend to believe in that moment?

    ----

3. What truth from Scripture corrects that lie?

    ----

4) Put Off and Put On Plan

Use the pattern from Ephesians 4:22–24.

Put off: What must I stop or resist?

Put on: What must I practice instead?

Renew: What truth will I repeat to my mind?

Now write one action step you will take in the next 48 hours.

My action step: ____

----

5) Active Dependence

Philippians 2:12–13 shows you work because God works.

1. What does it look like for you to "work out" obedience in your growth area?

    ----

2. What does it look like for you to depend on God while you work?

    ----

3. Who can support you through prayer or accountability?

    ----

6) Church and Growth

Answer honestly.

1. How connected are you to a local church right now?

    ----

2. What is one way you can pursue stronger Christian community this month?

    ----

3. What is one fear that keeps you from being known by others?

    ----

7) Respond to Failure

Think of a time you failed recently.

1. What was your first response?

    Examples: hiding, excuses, anger, despair, confession.

    ----

2. What would a better response look like next time?

    ----

3. What is one step you can take to reduce the chance of repeat failure?

Prayer Response

Write a prayer for growth. If you need help, complete these lines.

Father, Your will is my sanctification.

Thank You that sin is not my master in Christ.

Use Your Word to change my mind and desires.

Help me put off sin and put on obedience in ____________________ .

Give me strength to persevere when growth feels slow.

Amen.

Sanctification is God's lifelong work of shaping His people into a new way of life. It is real growth in holiness that happens through truth, effort, community, and grace.

CHAPTER 6

ASSURANCE AND ENDURANCE IN SALVATION

Many believers struggle with fear. They wonder if God will keep them. They wonder if their faith is real. They look at their failures and feel unsure. The Bible speaks to these fears with both comfort and clarity. God gives assurance to His people, and God calls His people to endure.

Assurance means confidence that you belong to Christ. It is not arrogance. It is not pretending you never doubt. It is steady trust based on God's promises and God's work in you. Endurance means continuing in faith. It means staying with Christ over time, through temptation, suffering, and seasons of weakness.

Assurance begins with God's character. God does not lie. God keeps His word. Titus 1:2 says God never lies (NSV). If God promises salvation to those who trust His Son, that promise is sure. Your assurance is not first built on your strength. It is built on God's faithfulness.

Assurance also rests on what Christ has done. Hebrews 7:25 says Jesus is able to save completely those who draw near to God through Him, since He always lives to intercede for them (NSV). This is strong comfort. Christ does not save halfway. He saves completely. He also prays for His people. Your salvation is not guarded by your grip on Christ alone. It is guarded by Christ's grip on you.

John 10:28–29 teaches that Christ gives eternal life and that no one can snatch His sheep from His hand (NSV). The Father is greater than all. This does not mean believers never struggle. It means the final outcome is secure because God is strong.

Still, many believers have shaky assurance. Why?

Sometimes assurance is weak because a person has never understood the gospel clearly. They think salvation is based on Christ plus their performance. That will always lead to fear. Scripture teaches salvation is by grace through faith. Works follow as fruit, not as the foundation.

Sometimes assurance is weak because of ongoing, unconfessed sin. Sin clouds the heart. It steals joy. It makes prayer feel heavy. It also dulls the conscience. A believer can still be saved and yet feel far from God because they are resisting Him. Confession restores fellowship and strengthens assurance.

Sometimes assurance is weak because of suffering or depression. A person may feel numb. They may feel abandoned. But feelings are not the final judge of truth. Psalm 42 shows a believer speaking to his own soul, calling himself to hope in God. The Bible makes room for real sadness, yet it calls believers to hold to God's promises.

Sometimes assurance is weak because of a tender conscience. Some believers are quick to see sin and slow to accept grace. They look inward too much. They measure salvation by their emotions. They need to look outward to Christ's work and to God's promises.

So how does Scripture say we can grow in assurance?

First, by trusting God's promises. 1 John 5:13 says these things are written so believers may know they have eternal life (NSV). God wants His people to know. Assurance is not a rare luxury. It is a normal gift God intends for believers.

Second, by looking for the fruit of new life. 1 John often points to signs of real faith, like obedience, love for other believers, and a pattern of turning away from sin. These signs do not earn salvation. They show it. Fruit is evidence, not the root.

Third, by using the means God provides. God strengthens assurance through Scripture, prayer, fellowship, the preaching of the Word, and the Lord's Supper. When believers neglect these, assurance often fades. When believers practice these with sincerity, assurance often grows.

Now we must also talk about endurance.

Scripture calls believers to continue. Colossians 1:23 speaks of continuing in the faith, stable and steadfast (NSV). Hebrews gives repeated warnings not to harden the heart. These warnings are real. They are part of how God keeps His people. God uses warnings to wake believers up and pull them back from danger.

Some people get confused here. They hear about security and endurance and think the Bible is contradicting itself. It is not. Scripture teaches both: God keeps His people, and God's people keep following. Endurance is not proof that you saved yourself. Endurance is proof that God is sustaining you.

Philippians 1:6 says God will bring to completion the good work He began (NSV). That is God's promise. Jude 24 says God is able to keep you from stumbling and present you blameless (NSV). That is God's power. At the same time, Hebrews 12:1 calls believers to run with endurance (NSV). That is your calling.

Endurance looks ordinary most of the time. It looks like praying when you feel tired. It looks like resisting sin when nobody is watching. It looks like keeping your promises. It looks like staying in the Word. It looks like staying in the church. It looks like returning to Christ after failure, not giving up.

Endurance also grows through testing. James 1 teaches that trials test faith and produce steadfastness (NSV). Again, this does not mean suffering is pleasant. It means God uses it. A tested faith becomes sturdier than an untested faith.

What if someone falls away?

Scripture teaches that some people appear to believe for a time, then leave. They may have religious activity, but their heart was never truly renewed. 1 John 2:19 says some went out because they were not truly of us (NSV). That verse is not meant to make believers paranoid. It is meant to urge honesty. It calls people to examine whether they truly trust Christ and whether their life shows a new direction.

At the same time, believers can stumble badly and still be restored. Peter denied Christ, yet Christ restored him. Failure is not the same as final apostasy. The difference is repentance. A true believer may fall, but will not stay content in sin. God brings His people back.

So how do you pursue assurance and endurance in a healthy way?

Start with Christ. Keep returning to what He has done. Then examine your life with honesty, not with panic. Confess sin quickly. Seek help when you are weak. Stay connected to a faithful church. Use God's Word daily. Pray for perseverance. Encourage other believers and receive encouragement.

Assurance and endurance are not meant to make you self-focused. They are meant to make you Christ-focused. The more you look to Christ, the more peace grows. The more you walk with Him, the more steady your faith becomes.

The goal is not a life without struggle. The goal is a life that keeps coming back to Jesus. God keeps His people, and His people endure. That is hope you can live on.

Workbook Section

1) Scripture Reading and Notes

Read each passage. Write one truth about assurance or endurance.

1. Titus 1:2 (NSV)

   ____

   ____

2. Hebrews 7:25 (NSV)

   ____

   ____

3. John 10:28–29 (NSV)

   ____

   ____

4. 1 John 5:13 (NSV)

   ____

   ____

5. Philippians 1:6 (NSV)

   ____

   ____

6. Hebrews 12:1 (NSV)

   ____

   ____

7. Jude 24 (NSV)

   ____

   ____

8. Colossians 1:23 (NSV)

----

2) What You Base Assurance On

Answer honestly.

1. When you feel unsure, what do you usually look at first?

   Examples: your feelings, your recent behavior, your past, God's promises.

   ----

2. What is dangerous about basing assurance only on feelings?

   ----

3. What is one promise from the passages above you can return to?

   ----

3) Signs of Life Check

These are not ways to earn salvation. They are possible evidences of new life.

Rate each from 1 to 5.

1 = weak right now, 5 = strong right now.

Desire to obey Christ:	1	2	3	4	5
Conviction when I sin:	1	2	3	4	5
Love for believers:	1	2	3	4	5
Desire for God's Word:	1	2	3	4	5
Willingness to repent:	1	2	3	4	5

Now write:

1. One area where you see God's grace at work.

    ----

2. One area where you need growth.

    ----

4) Confession and Renewal

If unconfessed sin is weighing on you, write it here in general terms.
The sin I need to confess is:

Write one step of repentance you will take.
My step:

Write one person you can ask to pray for you, if needed.
My support:

----

5) Endurance Plan

Hebrews 12:1 calls believers to run with endurance.

1. What is one "weight" that slows you down?
    Examples: distraction, bitterness, unhealthy habits, fear of people.

    ----

2. What is one "sin" that trips you often?

____

____

3. What is one practical change you will make this week?

____

____

4. What is one habit that helps you keep going?

____

____

6) When You Feel Weak

Write answers you can return to later.

1. When I feel weak, I will open: (choose one)
    A Bible passage:

____

____

A psalm:

____

____

A gospel account:

____

____

2. When I feel weak, I will pray this short prayer:
    Write a one-sentence prayer:

____

____

3. When I feel weak, I will reach out to:
    Write one person or group:

____

____

Write a prayer for assurance and perseverance. If you need help, begin here and finish it.

Father, thank You that You do not lie and You keep Your promises.

Lord Jesus, thank You that You save completely and intercede for Your people.

Help me rest in Your Word when I feel unsure.

Help me confess sin quickly and keep following You with endurance.

Keep me faithful until the end.

Amen.

Key Takeaway

Assurance rests on God's promises and Christ's finished work. Endurance is the ongoing path of faith. God keeps His people, and His people keep coming back to Him.

BOOK FOUR

LIVE BY THE SPIRIT GOD HAS GIVEN

God does not leave His people to live the Christian life by effort alone. He gives the Holy Spirit. The Spirit is not a mood, a force, or a vague feeling. He is God, and He works in real ways. This book will help you learn what Scripture teaches about the Spirit's person and power. You will study how He gives life, unites believers to Christ, grows fruit in daily character, and strengthens the church. Each chapter includes clear teaching and guided questions so you can depend on the Spirit with faith, wisdom, and steady obedience.

CHAPTER 1

THE SPIRIT IS GOD - NOT AN INFLUENCE

Teaching Section

Many people speak about the Holy Spirit as if He is a feeling. They may say, "I felt the Spirit," meaning they felt moved. Feelings can happen during worship, prayer, or repentance. But the Holy Spirit is not a feeling. He is not an "it." He is not an invisible energy. Scripture teaches the Spirit is a person, and the Spirit is God.

This matters because your view of the Spirit shapes your Christian life. If you think the Spirit is only a boost of emotion, you will chase moods. You will think God is near only when you feel warm inside. But if you know the Spirit is God, you will trust Him even when feelings are quiet. You will learn to depend on His truth and His presence in every season.

The Bible shows the Spirit is a person because He acts like a person.

First, the Spirit speaks and directs. In Acts 13:2, the Holy Spirit said to set apart Barnabas and Saul for the work God called them to (NSV). Speaking is personal action. Directing people is personal action. The Spirit is not a passive force.

Second, the Spirit has a will. 1 Corinthians 12:11 says the Spirit distributes gifts to each one as He wills (NSV). A will is not a cloud. A will belongs to a person who chooses and acts.

Third, the Spirit can be grieved. Ephesians 4:30 warns believers not to grieve the Holy Spirit of God (NSV). You cannot grieve electricity. You can grieve a person. The Spirit is personal, and He is holy.

Fourth, the Spirit teaches. 1 Corinthians 2:10 says the Spirit searches everything, even the depths of God (NSV). That same section explains that the Spirit knows God's thoughts. Knowing and teaching are personal actions.

The Bible also shows the Spirit is God.

In Acts 5:3–4, Peter confronts Ananias. He says Ananias lied to the Holy Spirit, then says he lied to God (NSV). Peter treats the Spirit as God, not as a created messenger.

2 Corinthians 3:17 says, "The Lord is the Spirit" (NSV). This does not erase the Father and the Son. It teaches the Spirit shares the divine nature. He is not less than God. He is the Lord.

The Spirit also has divine attributes. He is everywhere. Psalm 139:7 says there is no place you can flee from God's Spirit (NSV). Only God is present everywhere. The Spirit's presence is not limited by space.

The Spirit also does divine work. He is involved in creation. Genesis 1:2 says the Spirit of God was hovering over the waters (NSV). Creation is God's work. The Spirit is present and active in it.

The Spirit also gives life, which is God's work. Job 33:4 says the Spirit of God made the speaker, and the breath of the Almighty gives life (NSV). Giving life is not something a mere influence can do.

So why do people reduce the Spirit to an influence?

One reason is that people confuse the Spirit's work with emotions. The Spirit can bring conviction, joy, comfort, and awe. But feelings are not the Spirit Himself. Feelings rise and fall. The Spirit remains.

Another reason is that people fear being misled. Some have seen claims of "Spirit-led" behavior that ignored Scripture and harmed others. That is real harm. But the answer is not to shrink the Spirit into an idea. The answer is to honor the Spirit the way Scripture does. The Spirit never contradicts God's Word. He works through truth. He also produces holiness, not chaos.

Knowing the Spirit is God also protects you from a common mistake. Some people treat the Spirit as optional, as if serious Christianity is only about Jesus, and the Spirit is an extra. Scripture does not allow that. The Spirit is central to Christian life. No one comes to Christ without the Spirit's work. No believer grows without the Spirit's help.

Knowing the Spirit is a person also changes how you relate to Him. You do not use Him. You do not command Him. You do not treat Him like a tool. You honor Him. You listen. You ask for help with humility. You seek to please God, not to control spiritual experiences.

This also shapes your worship. Worship is not about getting a certain feeling. Worship is responding to God in truth. The Spirit helps you worship with sincerity. He opens your eyes to Christ. He presses God's truth into your heart. He strengthens faith when you feel weak.

It also shapes your obedience. When you are tempted, you do not need a rush of emotion to obey. You need truth, prayer, and strength. The Spirit supplies strength that is steady, not flashy. He helps you say no to sin and yes to righteousness. He helps you endure when life is hard.

So the main point is clear. The Holy Spirit is God, and He is a person. He is not an influence. He speaks, wills, teaches, and can be grieved. He is present everywhere. He gives life. When you know who the Spirit is, you can depend on Him with reverence and confidence.

Workbook Section

1) Scripture Reading and Notes

Read each passage. Write one clear observation from each.

1. Acts 13:2 (NSV)

   ____

   ____

2. 1 Corinthians 12:11 (NSV)

   ____

   ____

3. Ephesians 4:30 (NSV)

   ____

   ____

4. Acts 5:3–4 (NSV)

   ____

   ____

5. 2 Corinthians 3:17 (NSV)

   ____

   ____

6. Psalm 139:7 (NSV)

____

____

7. Genesis 1:2 (NSV)

____

____

8. Job 33:4 (NSV)

____

____

2) Person or Influence

Write "person" or "influence" next to each statement.

1. The Spirit teaches and guides.

____

____

2. The Spirit is a power I can control.

____

____

3. The Spirit can be grieved by sin.

____

____

4. The Spirit is just a worship feeling.

____

____

5. The Spirit chooses how gifts are given.

____

____

6. The Spirit is fully God.

____

Psalm 139:7 (NSV)_________________________

Now write one sentence explaining why it matters that the Spirit is a person.

My sentence:

----

3) Correct a Wrong Idea

Choose one wrong idea you have heard or believed.

Common wrong ideas:

- "The Spirit is a force."
- "The Spirit is only for certain Christians."
- "The Spirit always shows up as strong emotion."
- "The Spirit leads people away from Scripture."

The wrong idea I want to reject is:

Now correct it using one verse from today's list.

Verse and correction:

----

4) Reverence Check

Ephesians 4:30 says the Spirit can be grieved.

1. What kinds of sin tend to dull your spiritual sensitivity?

   Examples: harsh speech, secret compromise, bitterness, dishonesty.

   ----

2. What is one step of repentance you will take this week?

----

3. What is one habit that helps you walk in holiness?

----

5) Dependence Practice

Write short answers you can use in prayer.

1. One area where I need the Spirit's help today is:

----

2. One truth I will rely on is:

----

3. One choice of obedience I will make is:

----

4. One way I will seek God's Word today is:

----

6) Worship and Feelings

Answer honestly.

1. When you do not feel much in worship, what do you assume?

----

2. What is a better truth to hold based on Psalm 139:7?

----

3. Write one sentence you will remind yourself of next time feelings are low.

\---

\---

Prayer Response

Write a short prayer of honor and dependence. If you need help, complete these lines.

Holy Spirit, You are God, not an influence.

\---

\---

Forgive me for treating You lightly or ignoring You.

\---

\---

Teach me to listen to Your Word and obey with a willing heart.

\---

\---

Help me worship in truth, even when my feelings change.

\---

\---

Lead me in holiness today.

\---

\---

Amen.

Key Takeaway

The Holy Spirit is a real person and fully God. He speaks, wills, teaches, and can be grieved. Knowing who He is leads to reverent trust and steady dependence.

CHAPTER 2

THE SPIRIT BRINGS LIFE

The Christian life does not begin with a better attitude. It begins with new life. The Bible teaches that the Holy Spirit brings that life. Without the Spirit, a person can hear Bible words and still stay spiritually dead. A person can join a church, learn religious habits, and still lack true life with God. The Spirit changes that. He makes the gospel real to the heart.

Jesus explained this clearly when He spoke with Nicodemus. He said, "Unless one is born of water and the Spirit, he cannot enter the kingdom of God" (John 3:5, NSV). New birth is not a self-made upgrade. It is a work of God. The Spirit gives a kind of life that did not exist before. This is why Christianity is not first a set of rules. It is a rescue that includes a new heart.

Jesus also said, "That which is born of the flesh is flesh, and that which is born of the Spirit is spirit" (John 3:6, NSV). Flesh here points to human nature on its own. Humans can produce human efforts, but they cannot produce spiritual life. Only the Spirit gives spiritual life. The Spirit does not improve your old nature. He gives new life that begins a new direction.

This new birth is mysterious in its inner workings, but clear in its results. Jesus compared the Spirit's work to the wind. You cannot see the wind itself, but you can see its effects (John 3:8, NSV). In the same way, you may not be able to explain the exact moment your heart changed, but you can see the fruit. New life shows up in new desires. A person begins to care about truth. A person begins to feel conviction over sin. A person begins to hunger for God's Word. A person begins to love Christ and want to obey Him.

Titus 3:5 calls this work "the washing of regeneration and renewal of the Holy Spirit" (NSV). Regeneration means new birth. Renewal means a new direction of mind and heart. The Spirit cleans, not by scrubbing the outside only, but by changing what is inside. This is why salvation is not earned by good deeds. If the Spirit must bring life, then no one can boast.

The Spirit also brings life by giving spiritual sight. Without the Spirit, the gospel can seem dull or foolish. But when the Spirit opens a person's heart, Christ becomes precious. Sin becomes serious. Grace becomes amazing. That does not mean every believer feels strong emotion all the time. It means the Spirit changes what you value. He teaches you to see reality the way God sees it.

The Spirit's life-giving work is also seen in conversion. 1 Corinthians 6:11 speaks to people who once lived in many sins. Then it says, "But you were washed, you were sanctified, you were justified in the name of the Lord Jesus Christ and by the Spirit of our God" (NSV). That verse shows the Spirit's power to change real people with real pasts. The Spirit does not only forgive. He also sets apart. He also makes a new path possible.

The Spirit brings life in another important way. He strengthens believers to keep going. Romans 8:11 says the Spirit who raised Jesus from the dead dwells in believers, and He gives life to their mortal bodies (NSV). This points to present help and future hope. In the present, the Spirit strengthens you for obedience. In the future, the Spirit's presence guarantees resurrection life.

This matters because many believers try to live the Christian life with the wrong fuel. They try to change through shame, fear, or pure willpower. Shame might produce short bursts of effort, but it cannot produce lasting life. Fear can produce outward behavior, but it cannot produce a willing heart. Willpower can help with certain habits, but it cannot cleanse the conscience or remake the heart. The Spirit does what human effort cannot do.

This does not mean effort is useless. Believers are called to pursue holiness. But the order matters. The Spirit gives life first. Then effort becomes a response, not an attempt to earn God's favor. When the Spirit is the source, obedience can be steady. When self is the source, obedience becomes fragile.

So how do you know if the Spirit has brought life?

Do you trust Christ as your Savior and Lord? Do you have a growing awareness of sin and a desire to turn from it? Do you desire God's Word, even if your discipline is weak? Do you love God's people, even if you still struggle with selfishness? Do you keep coming back to Christ when you fail? These are signs of life. They are not reasons to brag. They are reasons to thank God.

What if you feel spiritually dry?

Dryness can happen for many reasons. Sometimes it comes from neglect of Scripture and prayer. Sometimes it comes from unconfessed sin. Sometimes it comes from suffering, grief, or depression. Dryness does not always mean you are lost. But it is a call to return to the means God uses. Open the Word. Pray simply. Seek help from mature believers. Confess known sin. Ask God for renewed strength.

The Spirit brings life, and that life is meant to grow. A newborn baby is alive, but still needs food, care, and time. In the same way, new spiritual life needs feeding. The Spirit uses Scripture to nourish faith. He uses prayer to grow dependence. He uses fellowship to strengthen endurance.

The main point is clear. The Holy Spirit brings life. He causes new birth. He renews the heart. He opens spiritual eyes. He strengthens believers to obey and to persevere. If you belong to Christ, you are not trying to create life from nothing. You are learning to live from the life the Spirit has already given.

Workbook Section

1) Scripture Reading and Notes

Read each passage. Then write one clear truth you learn about the Spirit bringing life.

1. John 3:5 (NSV)

----

2. John 3:6 (NSV)

----

3. John 3:8 (NSV)

   ----

4. Titus 3:5 (NSV)

   ----

5. 1 Corinthians 6:11 (NSV)

   ----

6. Romans 8:11 (NSV)

   ----

2) New Life in Your Own Words

Write a simple description.

New spiritual life means:

Now write one sentence that explains what new life is not.

New spiritual life is not:

   ----

3) Signs of Life Check

These are not a scorecard. They help you observe fruit.

Rate each from 1 to 5.

1 = weak right now, 5 = strong right now.

Desire to trust Christ:	1	2	3	4	5
Conviction when I sin:	1	2	3	4	5
Desire for Scripture:	1	2	3	4	5
Desire to pray:	1	2	3	4	5

Love for believers: 1   2   3   4   5
Willingness to repent: 1   2   3   4   5

Now write:

1. One area where you see evidence of life:

   ----

2. One area where you want growth:

   ----

4) Wind and Evidence

John 3:8 compares the Spirit's work to the wind.

1. What is one effect of the Spirit's work you can see in your life today?

   ----

2. What is one effect you want to see more clearly in the next month?

   ----

3. What is one habit that could support that growth?

   ----

5) From Dry to Fed

If you feel spiritually dry, answer these with honesty.

1. One possible cause of dryness for me is:

   Examples: distraction, fear, unconfessed sin, exhaustion, grief.

   ----

2. One step I will take this week to seek renewed strength is:

   ----

3.   One person I can ask for prayer or counsel is:

\---

\---

6) Washed and Renewed

Titus 3:5 speaks of washing and renewal.

1.   What is one old pattern you want God to wash away?

\---

\---

\---

\---

\---

2.   What is one new pattern you want God to grow in you?

\---

\---

\---

\---

\---

3.   Write one sentence of hope that you can say when you feel stuck.

\---

\---

\---

7) Prayer Response

Write a prayer asking God for life and renewal. If you need help, begin here and finish it.

Holy Spirit, thank You for bringing life where I could not.

\---

\---

Give me fresh desire for God's Word.

\---

\---

Expose what needs to change in my heart.

Strengthen me to repent and obey.

Help me live from the new life You have given.

Amen.

Key Takeaway

The Holy Spirit brings life through new birth and renewal. He changes the heart, opens spiritual sight, and strengthens believers to keep following Christ.

CHAPTER 3

THE SPIRIT UNITES BELIEVERS TO CHRIST

When a person is saved, God does more than forgive. He joins that person to Jesus Christ. This union is real. It is not a picture only. It is not a warm idea. It is a true spiritual connection created by the Holy Spirit. The Spirit unites believers to Christ so that what belongs to Christ becomes ours by grace.

This matters because many believers live as if Christianity is only trying harder. They think of Jesus as a helper on the outside. But Scripture describes something deeper. Christ lives in His people, and His people live in Him. That is union. The Spirit is the one who makes this union real and active.

1 Corinthians 6:17 says, "He who is joined to the Lord becomes one spirit with him" (NSV). This does not mean believers become divine. It means believers share a real spiritual bond with Christ. Through this bond, Christ's life becomes the source of the believer's life.

Romans 8:9 says, "Anyone who does not have the Spirit of Christ does not belong to him" (NSV). The Spirit is not optional. The Spirit is the mark of belonging. If you have the Spirit, you belong to Christ. If you belong to Christ, you have the Spirit. This union is not earned. It is given.

The Spirit unites believers to Christ in several key ways.

First, the Spirit joins us to Christ's death and resurrection. Romans 6:4 says believers were buried with Christ by baptism into death so that, just as Christ was raised, we too might walk in newness of life (NSV). This verse is about more than water. It is about what water points to. The Spirit joins you to Christ so that His death counts as your death to sin, and His resurrection becomes your new life.

This changes how you view sin. Sin is not your master anymore. You may still feel its pull, but you are not its property. You belong to Christ. Union means a change of ownership. You were under sin. Now you are under Christ.

Second, the Spirit makes Christ's benefits real in you. These benefits include forgiveness, peace with God, adoption, and hope. Ephesians 1:13 says believers were sealed with the promised Holy Spirit when they heard the word of truth and believed (NSV). A seal shows ownership and protection. The Spirit's presence is God's mark that you are His.

This sealing also serves as a guarantee. Ephesians 1:14 says the Spirit is the guarantee of our inheritance (NSV). That means your future with God is not a guess. The Spirit is like God's down payment, showing that He will finish what He started. You may feel weak, but God's promise is strong.

Third, the Spirit creates fellowship with Christ that changes daily life. Galatians 2:20 says, "It is no longer I who live, but Christ who lives in me" (NSV). Paul is not saying he disappeared. He is saying his old identity as self-ruler died. Christ now rules his life. This is a lived reality. Union changes what you want, how you decide, and what you pursue.

Fourth, the Spirit unites believers to Christ and also to each other. 1 Corinthians 12:13 says believers were all baptized by one Spirit into one body (NSV). The Spirit does not only create personal faith. He creates a people. He forms the church as Christ's body. This means union with Christ always has a community shape. If you belong to Jesus, you belong to His people.

This also challenges pride and isolation. Pride says, "I do not need others." Isolation says, "I will keep faith private." But the Spirit joins believers together. This does not mean church is always easy. It means church is part of God's design. The Spirit works through mutual care, correction, and encouragement.

Union with Christ also changes how you handle guilt. Many believers live with ongoing shame even after confession. They keep replaying failure. But union means you are not standing before God on your own. You stand in Christ. When God looks at you, He sees you in His Son. This does not excuse sin, but it does answer condemnation. Romans 8:1 says there is now no condemnation for those who are in Christ Jesus (NSV). "In Christ" is union language. The Spirit places you there.

Union also changes how you face suffering. If you belong to Christ, your suffering is not meaningless. You are not abandoned. God is present. Christ is with you. The Spirit comforts and strengthens. Romans 8:17 says believers are heirs with Christ, provided they suffer with Him in order that they may also be glorified with Him (NSV). This does not mean suffering earns glory. It means suffering is part of the path God uses, and union guarantees the end.

Union changes how you pursue holiness too. Growth is not about trying to become someone else. It is about living out what is already true. You are united to Christ, so you learn to live like you belong to Him. You fight sin because you are alive, not to become alive. You obey because you are accepted, not to become accepted.

So how do you live in light of union with Christ?

You remember who you belong to. You stop treating sin like a safe friend. You seek the help of the Spirit in prayer. You stay near God's Word because it tells you what is true. You stay connected to the church because the Spirit uses the body of Christ to strengthen you. You also learn to preach the gospel to yourself. When shame speaks, you answer with truth: you are in Christ, and the Spirit is the seal of that reality.

The main point is simple. The Holy Spirit unites believers to Christ. Through this union, Christ's death and resurrection shape your life. His benefits become yours. Your identity becomes steadier. Your hope becomes stronger. You are not trying to live the Christian life alone. You are living from your union with Jesus.

Workbook Section

1) Scripture Reading and Notes

Read each passage. Write one clear truth about union with Christ and the Spirit's role.

1. 1 Corinthians 6:17 (NSV)

    ____

    ____

2. Romans 8:9 (NSV)

    ____

    ____

3. Romans 6:4 (NSV)

----

4. Ephesians 1:13 (NSV)

----

5. Ephesians 1:14 (NSV)

----

6. Galatians 2:20 (NSV)

----

7. 1 Corinthians 12:13 (NSV)

----

8. Romans 8:1 (NSV)

----

2) Define Union in Plain Words

Finish the sentence.

Union with Christ means:

Now write one sentence that explains how the Spirit makes this union real.

The Spirit makes union real by:

----

3) Identity Check

Answer honestly.

1. When you fail, what do you tend to say about yourself?

    ____

    ____

2. How does Romans 8:1 correct your self-talk?

    ____

    ____

3. Write one truth statement you will repeat when guilt rises.

    ____

    ____

4) Ownership Change

Union means you belong to Christ.

1. What sin do you still treat like it belongs in your life?

    ____

    ____

2. What does Romans 6:4 call you to do instead?

    ____

    ____

3. What is one boundary you can set this week that matches your new ownership?

    ____

    ____

5) Sealed and Secure

Ephesians 1:13–14 speaks about being sealed.

1. What fears make you doubt God will keep you?

    ____

    ____

2. What does it mean that the Spirit is God's seal on you?

    ____

    ____

3. Write one sentence of assurance based on Ephesians 1:14.

----

6) Union and the Church

1 Corinthians 12:13 says the Spirit forms one body.

1. How connected are you to a local church right now?

----

2. What is one way you can pursue stronger connection in the next two weeks?

----

3. What is one barrier that keeps you from fellowship?

----

4. What is one step you will take to move past that barrier?

----

7) Daily Practice: Live From What Is True

Write a simple daily plan for the next seven days.

1. One short passage I will read each day is:

----

2. One prayer I will pray each day is:

----

3. One act of obedience that fits my union with Christ is:

----

4. One person I will encourage or reach out to is:

Write a prayer of gratitude and dependence. If you need help, begin here and finish it.

Father, thank You for uniting me to Christ by Your Spirit.

Thank You that I belong to Jesus and He lives in me.

Help me walk in newness of life and resist sin as a true response to grace.

Strengthen my faith when I feel weak.

Keep me close to Christ and close to His people.

Amen.

Key Takeaway

The Holy Spirit unites believers to Christ. This union changes identity, breaks sin's ownership, secures hope, and connects believers to the body of Christ.

CHAPTER 4

THE SPIRIT PRODUCES FRUIT, NOT JUST GIFTS

Many Christians talk about spiritual gifts. Gifts matter. God gives them for the good of the church. But Scripture puts strong focus on something else too: fruit. Fruit is the Spirit's work in your character. Gifts can be seen quickly. Fruit is seen over time. Gifts can draw attention. Fruit shows maturity.

A person can have visible gifts and still have a harsh spirit. A person can speak well and still lack self-control. A person can serve in public and still be proud in private. That is why the Bible points us to fruit. The Spirit does not only give ability. He forms a kind of person.

Galatians 5:22–23 lists the fruit of the Spirit: love, joy, peace, patience, kindness, goodness, faithfulness, gentleness, and self-control (NSV). This list is not a set of personality traits some people are born with. It is the Spirit's work in believers. It describes what the Spirit grows in a life that is learning to follow Christ.

Fruit is also connected to staying close to Christ. Jesus said, "Whoever abides in me and I in him, he it is that bears much fruit" (John 15:5, NSV). Fruit does not come from trying harder in your own strength. It comes from abiding. Abiding means staying close, staying dependent, staying connected. A branch does not strain to produce grapes. It stays connected to the vine, and life flows into it.

This helps us think about growth in a healthy way. Some believers try to change through fear and pressure. Others give up and assume they will never change. The Spirit offers a better path. You depend on Christ. You obey in small steps. You repent when you fail. Over time, the Spirit grows fruit that is real.

Now consider the difference between gifts and fruit.

Gifts are abilities given by God for service. Fruit is character shaped by God for holiness. Gifts are distributed in different ways. Not everyone has the same gift. Fruit is for every believer. No Christian is called to pursue "some" fruit and ignore the rest. The Spirit's fruit is meant to shape the whole person.

Gifts can also be present in immature believers. This may surprise some people, but it is true. A person can have a gift and still need deep growth. Fruit is a clearer sign of maturity. Fruit shows what rules the heart when nobody is watching.

Fruit also protects the church. A church can be impressed by talent and energy. But talent without fruit can lead to harm. Leaders and teachers must be marked by character. The Spirit's fruit helps keep the church safe and healthy.

Let's walk through the fruit of the Spirit in a practical way.

Love is active good for others. It is not only affection. It is seeking another person's good, even when it costs you. Love is patient in conflict. Love refuses bitterness. Love tells the truth with care.

Joy is not constant cheerfulness. Joy is deep gladness rooted in God. It can exist in sorrow. It does not depend on a perfect week. Joy grows when you remember God's mercy and trust His promises.

Peace is not the absence of problems. Peace is a settled heart that trusts God. Peace also shows up in how you handle conflict. A peaceful person is not always quiet, but they are not ruled by chaos.

Patience is long-suffering. It is staying steady under delay, weakness, or irritation. Patience does not explode quickly. It can endure frustration without cruelty.

Kindness is practical care. Kindness notices needs. Kindness uses words that heal instead of wound. Kindness is not weakness. It is strength used for another person's good.

Goodness is moral integrity. It is choosing what is right, even when it costs you. Goodness refuses hidden compromise. Goodness is sincere.

Faithfulness is reliability. It is keeping your word. It is being steady over time. Faithfulness shows up in marriage vows, work habits, church commitments, and private obedience.

Gentleness is controlled strength. Gentleness does not mean you never confront sin. It means you confront with humility, not harshness. Gentleness is careful with people who are weak.

Self-control is restraint. It is the ability to say no to wrong desires and yes to obedience. Self-control matters in speech, food, spending, sexuality, time, and anger. It is not grit alone. It is Spirit-enabled discipline.

Fruit grows through repeated choices. A tree does not produce fruit by trying once. It grows through seasons. In the same way, the Spirit grows fruit as you practice obedience again and again.

2 Peter 1:5–8 speaks about growth like this. It calls believers to make every effort to add virtue, knowledge, self-control, steadfastness, godliness, brotherly affection, and love (NSV). This does not contradict grace. It shows the shape of a responsive life. God gives life, and believers respond with effort that depends on God. Growth is not passive.

Philippians 1:9–11 also connects fruit to the Spirit's work. Paul prays that believers will abound in love with knowledge and discernment, so they approve what is excellent, and be filled with the fruit of righteousness that comes through Jesus Christ (NSV). That passage shows fruit has roots. Love grows with truth. Discernment grows with practice. Righteous fruit grows through Christ.

This is why the Spirit's fruit is so important for discernment. Many people try to measure spiritual life by dramatic moments. But fruit shows what is steady. A life that keeps producing love, patience, and self-control is showing the Spirit's work.

Fruit also helps you evaluate your use of gifts. Gifts should serve love. Gifts should build up others. If a gift makes you proud, it is being misused. If a gift becomes your identity, it becomes an idol. Fruit keeps gifts in their proper place.

Fruit also grows best in the soil of repentance. When the Spirit convicts you, do not hide. Confess sin. Turn from it. Ask God to reshape your desires. Repentance is not shame-driven self-punishment. It is returning to God with trust.

Fruit also grows in community. You cannot practice patience with nobody. You cannot practice gentleness in isolation. The church is one

160

place God uses to grow fruit, because it puts you near real people with real needs. That is where love becomes practical.

So what should you aim for?

Aim for a life that looks like Christ. Ask God for fruit more than attention. Ask Him for love more than applause. Ask Him for self-control more than comfort. Ask Him for gentleness more than the last word. Over time, the Spirit forms a steady Christian who can serve with gifts and also live with integrity.

The main point of this chapter is simple. The Spirit produces fruit that reflects Christ. Gifts matter, but fruit matters more. Fruit shows who you are becoming.

Workbook Section

1) Scripture Reading and Notes

Read each passage. Write one clear observation from each.

1. Galatians 5:22–23 (NSV)

    ----

2. John 15:5 (NSV)

    ----

3. 2 Peter 1:5–8 (NSV)

    ----

4. Philippians 1:9–11 (NSV)

    ----

5. Titus 2:11–12 (NSV)

    ----

2) Fruit Inventory

Rate each fruit from 1 to 5.

1 = weak right now, 5 = strong right now.

Love:	1	2	3	4	5
Joy:	1	2	3	4	5
Peace:	1	2	3	4	5
Patience:	1	2	3	4	5
Kindness:	1	2	3	4	5
Goodness:	1	2	3	4	5
Faithfulness:	1	2	3	4	5
Gentleness:	1	2	3	4	5
Self-control:	1	2	3	4	5

Now write:

1. Two fruits I thank God for today:

    ____

    ____

2. Two fruits I want to grow in the next month:

    ____

    ____

3) Abiding Practice

John 15:5 connects fruit to abiding.

Write a simple plan for the next seven days.

1. Time of day I will read Scripture:

    ____

    ____

2. Place where I will pray:

    ____

    ____

3. One distraction I will limit during that time:

    ____

    ____

4. One short prayer I will pray before reading:

4) Fruit in Conflict

Choose one recent conflict. Keep details general.

1. What fruit was hardest to show in that moment?

2. What did you do instead?

3. What would love plus truth look like next time?

4. Write one sentence you could say next time that shows gentleness.

5) Fruit in Private

Fruit is tested in private choices.

Choose one area where you need more self-control.

Examples: speech, spending, screen time, food, lust, anger, laziness.

My area:

Now write:

1. The usual trigger is:

2. The lie I tend to believe is:

----

3. A true statement from Scripture that corrects the lie is:

----

4. One boundary I will set this week is:

----

5. One replacement habit I will practice is:

----

6) Gifts and Fruit Together

Write short answers.

1. One gift or strength God has given me is:

----

2. One way I can use it to serve others is:

----

3. One fruit I need so this gift does not become pride is:

----

4. One step of humility I will take is:

----

7) Growth Plan With 2 Peter 1

Pick one quality named in 2 Peter 1:5–8 and set a plan.

The quality I will pursue is:

Two practical steps I will take this week:

1. ____

____

____

2. ____

____

____

One person I will ask to pray for me:

Write a short prayer. If you need help, complete these lines.

Holy Spirit, thank You for growing fruit in Your people.

____

____

Help me abide in Christ and depend on Him.

____

____

Grow love and self-control in me where I am weak.

____

____

Make my character steady so my service is safe and helpful.

____

____

Amen.

The Spirit does more than give gifts. He grows fruit. Fruit is Christlike character formed over time through abiding, repentance, truth, and steady obedience.

CHAPTER 5

THE SPIRIT BUILDS AND GUIDES THE CHURCH

God does not save people and then leave them alone. He gathers them. He forms a church. The church is not a club for like-minded people. It is the people of God, called out of sin and brought together in Christ. The Holy Spirit is the one who builds and guides this church.

Many believers think of the Spirit mainly in personal terms, like comfort, conviction, or strength for obedience. Those are real. But Scripture also shows the Spirit working in a public way through the church. The Spirit forms a people who worship, learn, serve, and grow together.

The Spirit builds the church in at least four clear ways: He gives unity, He gives gifts, He guides leadership, and He guards truth.

First, the Spirit gives unity.

Ephesians 4:3 calls believers to be "eager to maintain the unity of the Spirit in the bond of peace" (NSV). Unity is not something Christians create from scratch. The Spirit creates it by joining believers to Christ and to one another. Our job is to maintain it. That means we must protect unity from pride, gossip, and stubbornness.

Unity does not mean everyone thinks the same about every topic. It means believers share one Lord, one faith, one baptism, and one hope. It means we refuse to treat secondary issues as if they are more important than the gospel.

Unity also requires humility. Philippians 2:3–4 calls believers to do nothing from selfish ambition, but to count others more significant than themselves (NSV). Pride is one of the fastest ways to fracture a church. The Spirit builds unity through humble people who are willing to listen, repent, and forgive.

Second, the Spirit gives gifts for service.

1 Corinthians 12:4–7 says there are different gifts, but the same Spirit, and gifts are given for the common good (NSV). This means gifts are not badges for status. They are tools for love. God gives gifts so the church will be built up, cared for, taught, and strengthened.

Some gifts are more visible, like teaching. Others are less visible, like service, helps, or giving. Scripture teaches that every part of the body matters. A church becomes unhealthy when it praises certain gifts and ignores others. The Spirit gives a variety of gifts so that no one person becomes the center.

The Spirit also teaches believers to use gifts with love. 1 Corinthians 13 shows that gifts without love are empty. A person can speak well, but if they are harsh, their words do not build. A person can lead, but if they are proud, they harm. The Spirit's gifts must be guided by the Spirit's fruit.

Third, the Spirit guides the church through the Word and through qualified leaders.

The Spirit does not guide churches by sudden impressions that ignore Scripture. He guides through truth. Acts 20:28 says the Holy Spirit made overseers to care for the church of God (NSV). This shows the Spirit's role in appointing leaders. It also shows leaders have a sacred responsibility. They must shepherd God's people with care, not control.

The Spirit also equips leaders to teach sound doctrine and correct error. Titus 1:9 says a leader must hold firm to the trustworthy word, so he can give instruction and rebuke those who contradict it (NSV). The Spirit's guidance never pulls away from Scripture. The Spirit is the author of Scripture. He does not fight Himself.

Fourth, the Spirit guards the church by protecting truth and exposing error.

In Acts 15, the church faced a major doctrinal conflict. The leaders met, searched the Scriptures, and made a decision. Acts 15:28 says, "It has seemed good to the Holy Spirit and to us" (NSV). That line shows that the Spirit guided the church as they sought truth together. The Spirit did not give a secret revelation that replaced Scripture. He guided through the Word, prayer, and wise counsel.

The Spirit also guides the church in mission.

Acts 1:8 says believers will receive power when the Holy Spirit comes, and they will be witnesses (NSV). The Spirit strengthens believers to speak the gospel with courage and clarity. He also opens doors for ministry. He brings conviction to hearers. He draws people to Christ.

This does not mean every Christian is called to preach publicly. It means every Christian is part of a Spirit-empowered witness. The Spirit gives boldness, wisdom, and love for people who need Christ.

The Spirit also shapes the church's worship. Believers sing, pray, and hear Scripture. The Spirit works through these ordinary means. Sometimes worship feels powerful. Sometimes it feels quiet. Either way, the Spirit is present when God's people gather in truth.

So how should you respond to this teaching?

First, commit to the local church. If the Spirit builds the church, then the church matters. You cannot treat church as optional and still follow Scripture well. Online sermons can help, but they cannot replace real relationships, accountability, and shared life.

Second, serve with your gifts. Ask, "How can I build others up?" Do not wait for perfect conditions. Start small. Help where there is need. Use your time and skills for the good of the body.

Third, protect unity. Refuse gossip. Refuse unnecessary fights. Speak directly when needed. Be quick to forgive. Be slow to assume the worst.

Fourth, stay anchored in truth. Test teachings. Read Scripture. Learn sound doctrine. The Spirit uses truth to keep the church healthy.

Fifth, pray for leaders. Church leaders carry heavy responsibility. Pray they would be humble, wise, and faithful to Scripture. Pray they would not fear people. Pray they would not abuse power. Pray they would care for the weak and protect the church from error.

The main point is this: the Spirit builds and guides the church. He creates unity, gives gifts, appoints and equips leaders, guards truth, and strengthens mission. When you honor the Spirit's work in the church, you will grow and the church will be strengthened.

1) Scripture Reading and Notes

Read each passage. Write one clear observation from each.

1. Ephesians 4:3 (NSV)

   ----

2. 1 Corinthians 12:4–7 (NSV)

   ----

3. Acts 20:28 (NSV)

   ----

4. Acts 15:28 (NSV)

   ----

5. Acts 1:8 (NSV)

   ----

6. Philippians 2:3–4 (NSV)

   ----

7. Titus 1:9 (NSV)

   ----

2) Church Commitment Check

Answer honestly.

1. What has helped you stay connected to a local church?

   ----

2. What has made church connection hard for you?

    ----

3. What is one step you can take in the next two weeks to strengthen your involvement?

    ----

3) Unity and Peace

Ephesians 4:3 calls believers to maintain unity.

1. What usually threatens unity in your church setting?
   Examples: gossip, pride, unresolved conflict, factions, politics.

    ----

2. What role do you tend to play when conflict rises?
   Examples: avoider, fixer, fighter, silent critic, peacemaker.

    ----

3. What is one change you will make to protect unity?

    ----

4) Gifts for the Common Good

1 Corinthians 12 says gifts are for others.

1. One strength or gift I can use to serve is:

    ----

2. One need I see in my church or group is:

____

____

3. One way I can meet that need this month is:

____

____

4. What might keep you from serving?

____

____

5) Leaders and Care

Acts 20:28 speaks about leaders caring for the church.

1. What is one quality you should look for in church leadership?

____

2. What is one way you can support leaders in a healthy way?

____

3. Write a short prayer for your leaders.

____

6) Truth and Discernment

Titus 1:9 ties leadership to holding fast to the Word.

1. What is one false idea you have heard that sounds "Christian" but does not fit Scripture?

____

2. What is one practice that helps you stay grounded in truth?

____

3. What is one Bible habit you want to strengthen?

----

7) Mission and Witness

Acts 1:8 connects Spirit power to witness.

1. Who is one person you want to speak to about Christ?

----

2. What fear holds you back?

----

3. What is one step you can take this week?

   Examples: pray, invite, share a short testimony, offer to read Scripture together.

Prayer Response

Write a prayer for the church. If you need help, complete these lines.

Holy Spirit, thank You for building Christ's church.

Protect our unity and guard us from pride and division.

Help us use our gifts for the good of others.

Give our leaders wisdom and faithfulness to Your Word.

Make us bold witnesses with love and truth.
Amen.

Key Takeaway

The Spirit builds and guides the church by creating unity, giving gifts for service, equipping leaders, guarding truth, and empowering witness.

CHAPTER 6

WALKING BY THE SPIRIT DAILY

Many believers want to follow Christ, but they feel stuck. They know what is right, yet they struggle to do it. They start strong, then lose consistency. The Bible does not tell Christians to rely on willpower alone. It calls them to walk by the Spirit.

Galatians 5:16 says, "Walk by the Spirit, and you will not gratify the desires of the flesh" (NSV). This verse is both a command and a promise. It does not say believers will never feel temptation. It says believers do not have to obey temptation. The Spirit gives a new power and a new direction.

Walking by the Spirit is not a special experience for a few Christians. It is normal Christian life. It is not mystical. It is daily dependence on God, guided by Scripture, expressed through obedience.

To walk by the Spirit, you must understand what the "flesh" is. In Galatians 5, the flesh refers to the sinful nature that still pulls at the believer. It is the old pattern of life that wants to rule again. The flesh says, "Do what feels good now." The Spirit says, "Trust God and obey." The conflict is real. Galatians 5:17 explains that these desires are opposed (NSV). This is why you may feel torn inside. The answer is not to pretend the conflict is not there. The answer is to learn how to walk.

Walking is a picture of steady movement. It is not a leap. It is not a sprint. It is repeated steps in one direction. Walking by the Spirit means choosing the Spirit's path again and again.

Here are several practical parts of walking by the Spirit.

First, walking by the Spirit starts with believing what is true.

Romans 8:14 says those who are led by the Spirit of God are sons of God (NSV). If you belong to Christ, you are not trying to earn adoption.

You are living from it. When you forget who you are, you will live like the old self. When you remember you belong to God, you can resist sin with hope.

Second, walking by the Spirit means staying close to God's Word.

The Spirit never contradicts Scripture. He works through it. Colossians 3:16 says, "Let the word of Christ dwell in you richly" (NSV). A Spirit-led life is a Word-filled life. If Scripture is absent, you will rely on mood, impulse, or the opinions of others. Scripture gives a steady path when feelings shift.

This does not mean you must read huge amounts to be faithful. It means you must be consistent. A few verses each day, read with attention and prayer, will shape you more than occasional long sessions followed by neglect.

Third, walking by the Spirit means prayerful dependence.

Ephesians 6:18 calls believers to pray at all times in the Spirit (NSV). This does not mean non-stop talking. It means a posture of dependence. It means you ask for help before you are in trouble, not only after. It means you speak to God honestly when you feel weak. It means you bring temptation into the light through prayer.

Prayer can be short. It can be as simple as, "Lord, help me obey right now." The key is not fancy words. The key is real dependence.

Fourth, walking by the Spirit includes active obedience.

The Spirit helps you obey, but He does not obey for you. You still choose. You still turn from sin. You still take steps of wisdom. You still set boundaries. The Spirit empowers, guides, and strengthens, but you must walk.

This is why the Bible speaks about putting sin to death. Romans 8:13 says if by the Spirit you put to death the deeds of the body, you will live (NSV). Notice both parts. You put sin to death, and you do it by the Spirit. This is active dependence again. You fight, and God supplies power.

Fifth, walking by the Spirit means learning your patterns.

Many sins repeat because people ignore their triggers. Some are tempted when tired. Some are tempted when lonely. Some are tempted when angry. Some are tempted when bored. Wisdom pays attention. It does not excuse sin, but it prepares for battle. If you know your weak moments, you can plan for them. You can avoid certain settings. You can set limits on screens. You can call a friend. You can go to bed earlier. You can step away from conflict for a moment. These are not unspiritual choices. They are wise choices that support obedience.

Sixth, walking by the Spirit means staying in Christian community.

The Spirit builds the church for a reason. We need encouragement. We need correction. We need prayer. Hebrews 3:13 says believers should exhort one another daily so none are hardened by the deceitfulness of sin (NSV). Sin is deceitful. It tells lies that sound reasonable. Other believers can help you see what you cannot see.

Seventh, walking by the Spirit includes quick repentance.

When you sin, do not hide. Do not delay confession. Confession keeps your heart soft. Delay hardens the heart. A Spirit-led person is not sinless, but they are responsive. They do not make peace with sin. They return to God, ask for forgiveness, and take steps of change.

Walking by the Spirit also helps with decision-making.

Some believers want the Spirit to guide them by secret signs. Scripture points us to wisdom. Wisdom is Spirit-shaped thinking. It uses Scripture, prayer, counsel, and careful judgment. The Spirit often guides by shaping your desires toward what is good and by giving clarity through God's Word. When a choice involves sin, Scripture already answers. When a choice is morally neutral, wisdom helps you choose what is best.

Walking by the Spirit also guards you from pride.

A Spirit-led life does not produce boasting. It produces gratitude. When you obey, you thank God for help. When you fail, you return to Christ. The focus stays on God's grace, not on your record.

So what should you expect as you walk by the Spirit?

Expect a real fight. Expect slow growth in some areas. Expect stronger fruit over time. Expect that obedience becomes more natural as habits change and desires are trained. Also expect that God will use ordinary means, not only dramatic moments. A steady Christian life is often built through small choices made over years.

This chapter closes Book Four with a simple call. The Spirit is not only for the start of faith. He is for every day. Walking by the Spirit is daily dependence that shows up in truth, prayer, boundaries, repentance, and love. God does not ask you to live for Christ alone. He gives you the Spirit so you can follow with strength that is not your own.

Workbook Section

1) Scripture Reading and Notes

Read each passage. Write one clear truth about walking by the Spirit.

1. Galatians 5:16 (NSV)

    ____

    ____

2. Galatians 5:17 (NSV)

    ____

    ____

3. Romans 8:13–14 (NSV)

    ____

    ____

4. Colossians 3:16 (NSV)

    ____

    ____

5. Ephesians 6:18 (NSV)

    ____

    ____

6. Hebrews 3:13 (NSV)

    ____

    ____

2) What "Walking" Looks Like

Answer in simple words.

Walking by the Spirit means I will:

____

____

Now write one sentence that describes what walking by the Spirit is not.

It is not:

____

____

____

3) Daily Plan for the Next 7 Days

Write a plan you can keep.

1. Bible time:

   When: ____

   Where: ____

   How long: ____

2. Prayer plan:

   One short prayer I will use in temptation:

   ____

   ____

3. One obedience focus:

   The habit I want to practice this week:

   ____

   ____

4) Trigger and Boundary

Choose one sin you often struggle with. Keep it specific.

The sin pattern:

____

____

____

Now answer:

1. My common trigger is:

   ____

   ____

2. The lie I tend to believe is:

____

____

3. A truth from Scripture that corrects it is:

____

____

4. One boundary I will set this week is:

____

____

5. One replacement habit I will practice is:

____

____

5) Put Sin to Death by the Spirit

Romans 8:13 says you do this "by the Spirit."

1. What does active dependence look like for you in your struggle?

____

____

2. What is one step you can take today, not later?

____

____

3. Who can support you with prayer or accountability?

____

____

6) Community Step

Hebrews 3:13 calls believers to exhort one another.

1. One person I can reach out to this week is:

____

____

2. One way I can encourage them is:

____

____

3. One way they can help me stay honest is:

\-

\-

7) Quick Repentance Practice

If you have sinned recently, write a short confession in plain words.

I sinned by:

\-

\-

\-

I was wrong because:

\-

\-

\-

I ask God to forgive me through Christ because:

\-

\-

\-

I will take this step of change:

Prayer Response

Write a short prayer of dependence. If you need help, complete these lines.

Holy Spirit, I need Your help today.

\-

Lead me through Your Word and strengthen me to obey.

\-

Help me resist the desires of the flesh in_______________________ .

\-

Teach me to repent quickly and walk in a new direction.

\-

\-

Make my life steady and faithful, one step at a time.

Amen.

Key Takeaway

Walking by the Spirit is daily dependence that shows up in truth, prayer, obedience, wise boundaries, community, and quick repentance. The Spirit gives strength to resist sin and live a new way of life.

BOOK FIVE

HOLD FAST TO THE FUTURE GOD HAS PROMISED

God's promises about the future are not meant to satisfy curiosity. They are meant to strengthen faith and steady daily obedience. This book will help you learn what Scripture teaches about Christ's return, the resurrection, final judgment, and the life to come. It will also help you see how future hope shapes present choices, especially in suffering, temptation, and fear. Each chapter includes clear teaching and guided questions so you can hold fast to God's promises, live with watchful faith, and keep your hope anchored in what God will surely do.

CHAPTER 1

JESUS WILL RETURN IN POWER

Christians do not only look back to the cross and resurrection. They also look forward. Jesus will return. This is not a vague hope. It is a clear promise. The return of Christ is central to Christian faith because it completes God's plan in history. It brings justice, rescue, and renewal.

Acts 1:11 records an angel speaking to the disciples after Jesus ascended. The angel said Jesus will come in the same way they saw Him go into heaven (NSV). That promise ties Christ's return to real history. Jesus left in a real body. He will return in a real way. His return will not be an idea. It will be an event.

Jesus also taught that His return will be visible and powerful. Matthew 24:30 speaks of the Son of Man coming on the clouds of heaven with power and great glory (NSV). The point is not to map every detail. The point is certainty and majesty. Christ's return will not be hidden. It will not be small. It will reveal His authority over all.

The New Testament also teaches that Christ's return will be sudden. 1 Thessalonians 5:2 says the day of the Lord will come like a thief in the night (NSV). This does not mean Jesus is sneaky. It means His return will be unexpected to those who are not ready. People will be living ordinary life, making plans, assuming time will continue as usual. Then Christ will come.

Because the timing is unknown, Scripture calls believers to watchfulness. Jesus said, "You do not know on what day your Lord is coming" (Matthew 24:42, NSV). This is why the Bible does not encourage date-setting. It encourages readiness. The right question is not, "When will it happen?" The right question is, "Am I living faithfully today?"

Christ's return will also bring judgment. 2 Thessalonians 1:7–8 says the Lord Jesus will be revealed from heaven with mighty angels, in flaming fire, inflicting vengeance on those who do not know God and do not obey the gospel (NSV). This is serious. It shows that history has accountability. Evil will not go unaddressed forever. Christ's return will bring justice.

At the same time, Christ's return is comfort for believers. The same passage says Christ comes to be glorified in His saints (NSV). For those who belong to Christ, His return is not terror. It is rescue. It is the end of sin's presence. It is the end of death's threat. It is the end of the long struggle.

Titus 2:13 calls Christ's return "our blessed hope" (NSV). Hope in the Bible is not wishful thinking. It is confident expectation based on God's promise. The return of Christ is called blessed because it completes redemption. It means believers will see their Savior. It means faith will become sight.

Still, many believers do not think about Christ's return much. Some avoid it because it feels confusing. Some avoid it because it feels scary. Some avoid it because they are busy with life. But the Bible teaches that remembering Christ's return helps you live with clarity.

Here are three ways Christ's return shapes daily life.

First, it calls you to holiness. 1 John 3:3 says everyone who hopes in Christ purifies himself as Christ is pure (NSV). Hope has moral power. When you know you will stand before Christ, you take sin more seriously. You do not make peace with what Christ died to defeat.

Second, it steadies you in suffering. If life is painful, you may feel like evil is winning. But Christ's return guarantees that evil will not rule forever. God will set things right. This gives strength to endure without bitterness.

Third, it motivates faithful work. The Bible does not teach believers to stop living and wait passively. It teaches believers to live responsibly and serve with diligence, because Christ will return. Faithfulness now matters.

Christ's return will also expose what is hidden. Many injustices are never corrected in this world. Many lies are never admitted. Many faithful acts are never noticed. But Christ sees all. His return will reveal the truth. That should comfort the oppressed and warn the proud.

Christ's return will also gather God's people. 1 Thessalonians 4:16–17 speaks of the Lord descending, the dead in Christ rising, and believers being gathered to be with the Lord forever (NSV). That passage is meant to comfort grieving believers. It teaches that separation is not final for those in Christ.

So how should you respond?

Do not treat Christ's return as a topic for speculation. Treat it as a call to faithfulness. Live with clean hands and a steady heart. Keep short accounts with God. Confess sin quickly. Love your neighbor. Serve your church. Pray for endurance. Share the gospel with compassion. When Christ returns, you want to be found trusting Him and obeying Him.

The main point is clear. Jesus will return in power. His return will be visible, certain, and final. For those who reject Him, it brings judgment. For those who trust Him, it brings rescue and joy. Holding this hope shapes how you live today.

Workbook Section

1) Scripture Reading and Notes

Read each passage. Write one clear truth about Christ's return.

1. Acts 1:11 (NSV)

   ----

2. Matthew 24:30 (NSV)

   ----

3. Matthew 24:42 (NSV)

   ----

4. 1 Thessalonians 5:2 (NSV)

   ----

5. 2 Thessalonians 1:7–8 (NSV)

----

6. Titus 2:13 (NSV)

----

7. 1 John 3:3 (NSV)

----

8. 1 Thessalonians 4:16–17 (NSV)

----

2) Expectation and Readiness

Answer in short, honest sentences.

1. When you think about Jesus returning, what do you feel first?

----

2. Why do you think you feel that way?

----

3. What truth from today's passages steadies you most?

----

3) Watchfulness Check

Matthew 24:42 calls believers to watch.

1. What distractions most pull your heart away from readiness?
   Examples: busyness, entertainment, fear, money, anger, comfort.

------------Thessalonians-1:7–8-(NSV)------------------------

----

2. What is one change you can make this week to live more watchfully?

---

4) Holiness and Hope

1 John 3:3 links hope to purity.

1. What sin are you tempted to treat as "normal"?

---

2. What would repentance look like in one concrete step?

---

3. Who can support you in this change?

---

5) Comfort in Suffering

If you are in a hard season, answer these.

1. What is the hardest part right now?

---

2. How does the promise of Christ's return help you endure?

---

3. Write one sentence of hope you can say when you feel overwhelmed.

---

6) Faithful Work Until He Comes

Write short answers.

1. One responsibility God has placed in my hands right now is:

    ----

2. One way I can be more faithful in it this week is:

    ----

3. One person I can encourage with this hope is:

Prayer Response

Write a prayer of readiness and hope. If you need help, complete these lines.

Lord Jesus, thank You that You will return in power and glory.

Help me live ready, not careless.

Strengthen me to turn from sin and pursue holiness.

Comfort me and others with the promise that You will set all things right.

Keep me faithful until the day You come.

Amen.

Jesus will return in power. His return is certain, visible, and final. This hope calls believers to watchfulness, holiness, endurance, and faithful living.

CHAPTER 2

THE DEAD WILL BE RAISED

The Bible teaches that death is real, but it is not the end. God will raise the dead. This is not poetry only. It is a promise rooted in the resurrection of Jesus Christ. Christians do not hope in a vague afterlife. They hope in resurrection.

Resurrection means the body will live again. It is not the idea of a soul floating forever. It is not becoming an angel. It is not being absorbed into some higher spirit. Scripture teaches that God will raise people, and they will live in a real, renewed way.

The clearest teaching on resurrection is found in 1 Corinthians 15. Paul begins by reminding the church of the gospel. Christ died for our sins, was buried, and was raised (NSV). Then Paul draws a straight line from Christ's resurrection to ours. If Christ is raised, believers will be raised. If Christ is not raised, faith is empty and we are still in our sins.

1 Corinthians 15:20 says, "Christ has been raised from the dead, the firstfruits of those who have fallen asleep" (NSV). Firstfruits means the first part of a harvest that guarantees the rest. Christ's resurrection is the beginning of the harvest. The rest of the harvest is the resurrection of His people. This gives strong assurance. Your future is tied to Christ's victory.

Jesus also taught resurrection clearly. In John 5:28–29, He said that an hour is coming when all who are in the tombs will hear His voice and come out (NSV). That is an authority statement. Jesus has power over death. He will call the dead, and they will rise. The verse also says there will be a resurrection to life and a resurrection to judgment. Resurrection is not only for believers. All will be raised. The difference is what follows.

This truth is both comforting and sobering.

It is comforting because death does not win. Many believers have buried loved ones. Many have faced death themselves. Resurrection means separation is not final for those who are in Christ. It also means the body is not worthless. God made the body. Sin and death harmed it. God will redeem it. That is part of salvation.

It is sobering because resurrection includes accountability. People will not disappear. They will stand before God. Life is not a closed system. History has an ending, and every person will face the truth.

So what will resurrection be like?

1 Corinthians 15 explains that the resurrection body will be changed. Paul uses the picture of a seed. A seed is planted, and what grows is connected, yet transformed. He says the body is sown in weakness and raised in power (NSV). He also says it is sown perishable and raised imperishable (NSV). That means the resurrection body will not decay. It will not break down. It will not be headed toward death again.

Paul also calls the resurrection body "spiritual" (NSV). That word can be misunderstood. It does not mean non-physical. It means a body fully animated and directed by the Spirit, free from sin's corruption. Jesus' own resurrection helps us understand this. After His resurrection, Jesus could be seen, touched, and recognized. He ate food. He spoke. He was not a ghost. He was bodily alive. Yet His body was also transformed, no longer subject to death.

Resurrection also connects to creation. Romans 8:23 says believers groan as they wait for adoption as sons, the redemption of our bodies (NSV). Notice the phrase redemption of our bodies. Redemption is not escape from the body. Redemption is the body being made new and free from decay.

This helps correct two common errors.

One error is to treat the body as everything. Some people live as if the body is the highest good, so comfort and pleasure become the goal. That leads to idolatry.

The other error is to treat the body as nothing. Some people act as if the body is a shell and what you do in the body does not matter. That leads to sin and dishonor.

The Bible teaches a balanced truth. The body matters, and it will be raised. What you do with your body matters, because it belongs to God. Resurrection hope encourages holiness. You do not treat the body as a toy. You treat it as a gift and a trust.

Resurrection hope also strengthens endurance. 1 Thessalonians 4:13–14 says believers should not grieve as those without hope, because God will bring with Jesus those who have fallen asleep in Him (NSV). This does not cancel grief. Grief is real. But grief is not hopeless. Christians grieve with expectation.

Resurrection hope also helps you face suffering. Pain can make people feel trapped. Disease can make people fear the future. Aging can make people feel loss. Resurrection says, "This is not the final form." The present body is fragile. The future body will be raised and made whole. That hope does not remove sorrow, but it gives strength.

Resurrection also helps you live with courage. If death is not the end, you do not have to live in fear. You can do hard things. You can obey God when it costs you. You can serve others even when it is inconvenient. You can speak truth even when it brings opposition. Resurrection hope frees you from slavery to self-protection.

So how should you hold this truth?

Hold it with gratitude. Christ's resurrection is your guarantee. Hold it with humility. Resurrection is God's act, not human achievement. Hold it with holiness. If God will raise your body, honor Him with your body now. Hold it with comfort. Your loved ones in Christ are not lost. They are waiting. Hold it with urgency. All will be raised, and all will face God.

The main point of this chapter is clear. The dead will be raised. Christ's resurrection guarantees it. Believers will be raised to life, with bodies transformed and made whole. This hope strengthens faith, steadies grief, and shapes how we live today.

1) Scripture Reading and Notes

Read each passage. Write one clear truth about resurrection.

1. 1 Corinthians 15:20 (NSV)

    ----

2. John 5:28–29 (NSV)

    ----

3. 1 Corinthians 15:42–44 (NSV)

    ----

4. Romans 8:23 (NSV)

    ----

5. 1 Thessalonians 4:13–14 (NSV)

    ----

6. Philippians 3:20–21 (NSV)

    ----

2) Define Resurrection

Write a simple definition.

Resurrection means:

Now write one sentence that says what resurrection is not.

Resurrection is not:

----

3) Firstfruits and Assurance

1 Corinthians 15:20 calls Christ "firstfruits."

1. What does firstfruits mean in your own words?

    ----

2. How does this give confidence about your future?

    ----

3. Write one sentence you can say when fear of death rises.

    ----

4) Grief With Hope

If you have lost someone, you may answer these. If not, answer as preparation.

1. What do you most fear about death or loss?

    ----

2. How does 1 Thessalonians 4:13–14 correct that fear?

    ----

3. What is one way you can comfort someone else with this hope?

    ----

5) Body Honor Check

Romans 8:23 speaks of the redemption of our bodies.

1. Do you tend to treat your body as everything, or as nothing, or as a gift?

    ----

2. What is one way you can honor God with your body this week?

3. Examples: purity, rest, self-control, caring for health, refusing harmful habits.

4. What is one habit that dishonors God with your body?

5. What is one boundary you will set to fight that habit?

6) Live With Courage

Answer with concrete steps.

1. What is one obedience step you have delayed because of fear?

2. How does resurrection hope give you courage to do it?

3. What is one step you will take in the next 48 hours?

Write a prayer of hope. If you need help, complete these lines.

Father, thank You that death is not the end.

\---

\---

Thank You that Christ's resurrection guarantees the resurrection of His people.

\---

\---

Comfort those who grieve and strengthen those who fear.

\---

\---

Help me honor You with my body and live with courage and hope.

\---

\---

Keep my eyes on the life to come.

\---

\---

Amen.

Key Takeaway

The dead will be raised. Christ's resurrection is the guarantee. This hope comforts grief, strengthens courage, and shapes a holy life in the present.

CHAPTER 3

HEAVEN AND HELL ARE REAL AND FINAL

The Bible teaches that every human life has an end, and every human life also has an eternal outcome. Heaven and hell are real. They are not symbols. They are not myths meant to scare people into behaving. They are part of God's final judgment and final mercy. Scripture speaks about them with clarity and seriousness because eternity is not a small topic.

Many people prefer to avoid this subject. Some think it is too heavy. Some think it is unkind. Some think it is embarrassing. But the Bible does not treat it that way. Jesus spoke about final judgment more than many people realize. He did not do it to entertain curiosity. He did it to warn, to call for repentance, and to offer real hope.

Heaven is the final home of those who belong to Christ. Hell is the final judgment for those who reject God. Both are final. There is no second death for believers, and there is no later escape for those judged. This truth makes the gospel urgent and precious.

Let's begin with heaven.

Heaven is described as being with the Lord. Revelation 21:3 says God's dwelling will be with His people, and He will be their God (NSV). That is the heart of heaven. It is not mainly about comfort. It is about communion. The greatest gift is God Himself.

Heaven is also described as a place without sin and without death. Revelation 21:4 says God will wipe away every tear, and death will be no more, and mourning and pain will be gone (NSV). This is not temporary relief. It is final healing. Sin will not threaten peace again. Death will not return. Loss will not repeat.

Heaven is also described as joyful worship. Revelation 7:9–10 shows a great multitude from every nation praising God and the Lamb (NSV).

This shows heaven is not dull. It is full of life. Worship there is not forced. It is the natural response of redeemed people who finally see God's glory without the fog of sin.

Heaven is also described as inheritance. 1 Peter 1:4 says believers have an inheritance that is imperishable, undefiled, and unfading, kept in heaven (NSV). That means it cannot be stolen. It cannot rot. It cannot be lost. This gives security. What God promises is safe.

Now we must speak about hell.

Hell is real, and it is final. Scripture describes it as judgment, separation from God's favorable presence, and conscious punishment. 2 Thessalonians 1:9 says those who do not obey the gospel will suffer the punishment of eternal destruction, away from the presence of the Lord and from the glory of His might (NSV). That verse stresses both punishment and separation.

Jesus also spoke of final judgment in Matthew 25:46. He said some will go away into eternal punishment, but the righteous into eternal life (NSV). Notice the parallel. The same word eternal describes both outcomes. Jesus presents two final destinations with lasting results. This is why the church has always taken hell seriously.

Some people ask, "How can a good God allow hell?" Scripture gives several truths that help us think rightly.

First, God is just. Justice means God does what is right. If God never judged evil, He would not be morally good. Many people demand justice when they are harmed. They want wrongs to be answered. Hell shows that evil matters and God's court is not asleep.

Second, sin is serious. Sin is not only harming others. It is rebellion against God. It is refusing God's rightful rule. The weight of sin is measured by the One sinned against. God is holy and infinite in worth. Sin against Him is not trivial.

Third, hell is not God losing control. It is God judging in truth. Judgment is not an emotional outburst. It is a settled verdict from the righteous Judge.

Fourth, God offers mercy. The Bible does not present hell without also presenting the gospel. God warns so people will flee to Christ. Ezekiel 33:11 says God takes no pleasure in the death of the wicked, but that the wicked turn from his way and live (NSV). God's warning is a form of mercy.

Fifth, people are responsible. Scripture presents unbelief as willful. People love darkness rather than light. They refuse to come to Christ. Hell is not a trap God hides. It is the end of chosen rebellion.

Another question people ask is, "Will everyone finally be saved?" Some hope so, but Scripture does not teach it. Jesus speaks of a narrow gate and a hard way that leads to life, and a wide way that leads to destruction (Matthew 7:13–14, NSV). This is not meant to make believers proud. It is meant to call people to repentance.

Another question is, "Do Christians go to heaven when they die, or do they wait for the resurrection?" Scripture points to both present comfort and future fullness. Believers who die are with the Lord in a real sense. Yet the final state includes resurrection and the new creation. Heaven is not only a disembodied existence. The Bible's final picture includes a renewed world where God dwells with His people.

So how does this teaching shape life now?

It shapes your priorities. If heaven is real, you do not live for temporary approval alone. Colossians 3:2 says to set your mind on things above (NSV). That does not mean you neglect responsibilities. It means you keep eternal values in view.

It shapes your comfort. If you are suffering, Revelation 21:4 gives true hope. Pain is not forever for those in Christ. Tears will end. Death will end. God will heal.

It shapes your urgency. If hell is real and final, people need the gospel. Love does not stay silent when the danger is real. This does not mean you preach with harshness. It means you speak with humility and compassion, remembering you are saved by grace.

It shapes your worship. If you understand what you have been saved from and what you have been saved to, gratitude grows. Worship becomes more sincere.

It also shapes your view of justice. When you see evil that seems unpunished, you do not need to take vengeance into your own hands. God will judge. That frees you to pursue justice in lawful ways, but not with bitterness.

The main point is this. Heaven and hell are real and final. Heaven is the home of God's people, marked by God's presence, joy, and the end of death. Hell is God's just judgment on sin, marked by separation and lasting punishment. This truth calls you to repentance, faith, humility, and compassionate witness.

Workbook Section

1) Scripture Reading and Notes

Read each passage. Write one clear truth about heaven or hell.

1. Revelation 21:3–4 (NSV)

    ----

2. 1 Peter 1:4 (NSV)

    ----

3. Revelation 7:9–10 (NSV)

    ----

4. Matthew 25:46 (NSV)

    ----

5. 2 Thessalonians 1:9 (NSV)

    ----

6. Ezekiel 33:11 (NSV)

    ----

7. Matthew 7:13–14 (NSV)

    ----

8. Colossians 3:2 (NSV)

    ----

2) Two Real Destinations

Write two short statements.

Heaven is real because:

____

____

____

Hell is real because:

____

____

____

Now write one sentence that explains why both matter for the gospel.

They matter because:

____

____

____

3) What You Expect From Heaven

Answer in clear sentences.

1. What do you most look forward to about being with the Lord?

    ____

    ____

2. Which promise in Revelation 21:3–4 comforts you most?

    ____

    ____

3. How should this hope shape your choices this week?

    ____

    ____

4) Respond to the Warning

Matthew 25:46 speaks of eternal outcomes.

1. What does this passage teach you about the seriousness of sin?

    ____

    ____

2. What does it teach you about God's justice?

----

3. What does it teach you about the need for the gospel?

----

5) Compassionate Witness

Think of one person who does not know Christ.

1. What makes it hard to speak to them about spiritual things?

----

2. What fear holds you back?

----

3. What is one kind and clear step you can take in the next seven days?

    Examples: pray with them, ask a question, share a short testimony, offer to read Scripture.

----

4. Write one sentence you could say that is truthful and gentle.

6) Set Your Mind Above

Colossians 3:2 calls you to set your mind on things above.

1. What earthly thing most steals your focus?

----

2. What is one habit that would help you reset your focus daily?

----

3. What is one practical way you can store up eternal value this week?

Examples: serving, giving, forgiving, sharing the gospel.

Write a prayer that holds both hope and seriousness. If you need help, complete these lines.

Father, thank You for the sure hope of being with You forever.

Thank You that You will wipe away tears and end death.

Help me take Your warnings seriously and turn from sin.

Give me compassion for those who do not know Christ.

Help me speak truth with humility and love.

Amen.

Heaven and hell are real and final. Heaven is life with God, with sin and death removed. Hell is God's just judgment on sin. This truth shapes worship, priorities, and compassionate witness.

CHAPTER 4

GOD WILL MAKE ALL THINGS NEW

The Bible's final hope is not escape from the world. It is renewal. God will make all things new. This is not a small touch-up. It is a complete restoration of what sin has damaged. God will remove evil, heal what is broken, and bring His people into a renewed creation where righteousness dwells.

Revelation 21:5 says, "Behold, I am making all things new" (NSV). That sentence is spoken from the throne. It is God's promise. It does not say, "I am making some things better." It says all things new. This points to God's power and God's plan.

This truth matters because many believers feel tired. They see death, sickness, injustice, and conflict. They wonder if anything will ever truly change. Scripture says yes. Change is coming, and it will be God's work. The future is not a human project. It is God's final act.

To understand renewal, we need to see what sin did.

Sin brought disorder. It broke fellowship with God. It corrupted human hearts. It brought decay into the created world. Romans 8:20–21 says creation was subjected to futility and is in bondage to corruption, but it will be set free (NSV). This is important. Creation itself is waiting for liberation. God's plan includes the created order, not just human souls.

Renewal also includes the end of the curse. Revelation 22:3 says, "No longer will there be anything accursed" (NSV). That means what sin brought into the world will be removed. The world will no longer be marked by frustration, decay, and death. Work will no longer be painful in the same way. Relationships will no longer be poisoned by selfishness. The curse will be gone.

Renewal also includes the visible presence of God among His people. Revelation 22:4 says God's servants will see His face (NSV). This is stunning. In the present age, we walk by faith. We see God's goodness through His Word and His works. In the new creation, there will be direct fellowship without the barrier of sin. God will not feel distant. His presence will be clear and constant.

This renewed future is tied to Christ's victory. Colossians 1:19–20 says God was pleased to reconcile all things to Himself, making peace by the blood of Christ's cross (NSV). "All things" includes people and creation. The cross is not only the answer to personal guilt. It is the foundation of cosmic restoration. Christ's work is wide enough to heal what sin shattered.

This also means the future is physical and real. The Bible speaks of a new heaven and a new earth. It speaks of life with God in a renewed world. Some believers have been taught to think heaven means floating in the clouds forever. Scripture gives a fuller picture. God's people will live in God's renewed world, with resurrected bodies, in a life marked by holiness and joy.

2 Peter 3:13 says, "According to his promise we are waiting for new heavens and a new earth in which righteousness dwells" (NSV). Righteousness dwelling means it is at home there. Sin will not be tolerated. Evil will not return. The new creation will be the right world, ordered under God, filled with peace.

This future also answers a deep longing in the human heart. People long for justice, beauty, safety, and lasting love. Those desires often get twisted, but the longing itself points to something real. We were made for God's world as it was meant to be. The new creation is that world, restored and purified.

But how does God make all things new?

Scripture shows two key parts.

First, God removes evil. He judges sin. He defeats the final enemies. Death is called the last enemy to be destroyed (1 Corinthians 15:26, NSV). God does not coexist with evil forever. He brings it to an end.

Second, God restores what is good. He heals. He renews. He brings His people into a life where worship and work are pure and joyful. In the new creation, serving God is not a burden. It is a delight.

This truth also protects you from despair. You may work for justice now and still see limited results. You may fight sin and still feel weakness. You may lose people you love. You may see brokenness that cannot be fixed in this life. Renewal means your labor is not wasted. God will finish what you cannot.

It also protects you from idolatry. Some people place all hope in progress, politics, or technology. Others place all hope in personal comfort. Scripture says do good now, but do not place ultimate hope in this age. Only God can bring final renewal.

Renewal also shapes how you view suffering. Suffering is not the final word. Romans 8:18 says present sufferings are not worth comparing with the glory to be revealed (NSV). That does not minimize pain. It places pain in a larger story. The coming renewal is so great that it will put present sorrow in its place.

Renewal also shapes how you treat creation. If God plans to renew creation, then creation matters. Christians should not treat the world as disposable. We should act as good stewards. We cannot save the world by our effort, but we can honor God by caring for what He made. Stewardship is part of love for God and neighbor.

Renewal also shapes the church's mission. We do not preach only "escape." We preach reconciliation with God through Christ. We invite people into a future with God. We also show signs of that future now through acts of mercy, truth, justice, and love. These acts do not create the new creation, but they point toward it.

So how do you live with this promise?

You hold it in your mind when the world feels heavy. You remind yourself that God is not finished. You choose faithfulness in small tasks. You repent of sin because it will not fit the coming world. You serve others because love belongs to God's future. You keep worship steady because God will dwell with His people.

The main point is clear. God will make all things new. The curse will end. Creation will be set free. God will dwell with His people in a renewed world where righteousness is at home. This promise gives endurance, steadies sorrow, and shapes faithful living today.

1) Scripture Reading and Notes

Read each passage. Write one clear truth about God's renewal.

1. Revelation 21:5 (NSV)

    ____

    ____

2. Romans 8:20–21 (NSV)

    ____

    ____

3. Revelation 22:3–4 (NSV)

    ____

    ____

4. 2 Peter 3:13 (NSV)

    ____

    ____

5. Colossians 1:19–20 (NSV)

    ____

    ____

6. 1 Corinthians 15:26 (NSV)

    ____

    ____

7. Romans 8:18 (NSV)

    ____

    ____

2) Define "All Things New"

Write a simple definition.

God making all things new means:

____

____

____

Now write one sentence that explains what this promise does not mean.

It does not mean:

____

____

____

3) Hope for a Tired Heart

Answer honestly.

1. What part of the world's brokenness weighs on you most?

____

____

2. Which promise from today's passages speaks to that weight most clearly?

____

____

3. Write one sentence of hope you can repeat when you feel discouraged.

____

____

4) Renewal and Repentance

If God will bring a world where righteousness dwells, sin does not fit.

1. What sin do you need to stop treating as "small"?

____

____

2. What is one step of repentance you will take this week?

____

____

3. What is one replacement habit you will practice instead?

____

____

5) Stewardship in the Present

Romans 8 says creation will be set free.

1. What is one way you can care for what God has made this week?

    Examples: reduce waste, act responsibly at work, care for your home, avoid careless harm.

    ----

2. What is one way you can show love for your neighbor through practical care?

    ----

6) Signs of the Coming World

Write two ways your life can point to God's coming renewal.

1. One act of mercy I will do this week is:

    ----

2. One act of truth and integrity I will do this week is:

Prayer Response

Write a prayer of hope and faithfulness. If you need help, complete these lines.

Father, thank You that You will make all things new.

When I feel tired, remind me that You are not finished.

Help me repent of sin that does not fit Your coming world.

Teach me to serve and steward with hope, not despair.

Keep my eyes on the day when righteousness will dwell and the curse will end.

Amen.

Key Takeaway

God will make all things new. He will end the curse, free creation from corruption, and dwell with His people in a renewed world where righteousness is at home.

CHAPTER 5

LIVE TODAY IN LIGHT OF THE END

Teaching Section

God's promises about the end are not given so we can argue over timelines. They are given so we can live wisely now. The future shapes the present. If you believe Jesus will return, the dead will be raised, and God will judge and renew all things, then your daily choices matter. You are not drifting. You are moving toward a real meeting with God.

The Bible often connects end-time truth to daily faithfulness. One clear example is 2 Peter 3:11. After speaking about the day of the Lord, Peter asks, "What sort of people ought you to be in lives of holiness and godliness?" (NSV). He does not say, "What charts should you draw?" He says, "What kind of life should you live?" The end should make you serious about holiness and steady obedience.

Living in light of the end begins with watchfulness. Jesus said, "Be ready, for the Son of Man is coming at an hour you do not expect" (Matthew 24:44, NSV). Readiness is not panic. It is steady faithfulness. It means keeping your heart soft, your conscience clean, and your priorities aligned with God's will.

Watchfulness also means you do not fall asleep spiritually. Many people live as if life will always stay the same. They assume they will have endless time to change, to repent, to reconcile, or to obey. Scripture calls that foolishness. James 4:14 says you do not know what tomorrow will bring, and life is like a mist (NSV). That is not meant to make you afraid. It is meant to make you wise.

Living in light of the end also means living with holiness. Holiness is not being strange. Holiness is being set apart for God. It is living in a way that matches His character. 1 Peter 1:15–16 says, "As he who called you is holy, you also be holy in all your conduct" (NSV). The end time hope that God will remove sin should make you want to remove sin now, not make peace with it.

Holiness includes private choices. It includes what you do when nobody is watching. It includes what you click, what you say, what you imagine, and what you hide. Living in light of the end means you stop treating hidden sin as safe. God sees it. The end will expose what is hidden. Wisdom confesses now.

This future hope also shapes relationships. If you know you will stand before God, you will take love and forgiveness seriously. Romans 12:18 says, "If possible, so far as it depends on you, live peaceably with all" (NSV). You cannot control others, but you can pursue peace with humility and truth. You can refuse revenge. You can seek reconciliation where possible. You can speak honestly without cruelty.

Living in light of the end also changes how you use time and money. Temporary things are real, but they are not ultimate. Jesus taught people to store up treasure in heaven, where it cannot be destroyed or stolen (Matthew 6:19–20, NSV). He does not forbid possessions. He forbids worshiping them. He calls you to invest in what lasts.

This affects daily spending. It affects generosity. It affects how you use free time. It affects what you chase. It calls you to ask, "Will this matter in eternity?" Not every activity must feel spiritual. Rest and enjoyment are gifts. But the end calls you to avoid wasting your life on what cannot satisfy.

Living in light of the end also shapes your work. Colossians 3:24 says you serve the Lord Christ (NSV). That means your job is not only for income. It is an assignment from God. Even small tasks can be done in faith. The end reminds you that God sees hidden labor. Faithful work done with integrity is not wasted.

This future hope also shapes your witness. If heaven and hell are real and final, then people need the gospel. Love speaks. Paul says in 2 Corinthians 5:10–11 that we must all appear before the judgment seat of Christ, and therefore we persuade others (NSV). Persuading does not mean manipulating. It means speaking with clarity and care because the stakes are real.

The end also shapes how you handle suffering. When pain comes, it can tempt you to bitterness or despair. But the end reminds you that pain is not forever. God will make all things new. That hope helps you endure with patience. It also helps you keep doing good even when life is hard.

Living in light of the end also protects you from two common errors.

The first error is obsession. Some people become consumed with end-time details. They chase predictions and arguments. They become anxious or proud. Scripture calls for readiness, not obsession. The end should lead to obedience, not endless speculation.

The second error is neglect. Some people ignore the future entirely. They live as if Jesus will not return. They drift into comfort and distraction. Scripture calls that spiritual sleep. The end is meant to wake you up.

So what does a faithful life look like in light of the end?

It looks like daily repentance. It looks like prayer and Scripture. It looks like faithful church life. It looks like honest work. It looks like love for neighbor. It looks like generosity. It looks like resisting sin and practicing holiness. It looks like hope in suffering. It looks like speaking the gospel with gentleness and respect.

You do not need to do all of this perfectly. You need to keep turning toward Christ. The end is not meant to crush you. It is meant to clarify what matters. It is meant to pull you out of trivial living. It is meant to strengthen you for steady faithfulness.

The main point is simple. The end is certain, so live faithfully now. Christ will return. Judgment will come. Renewal will arrive. Let that future shape your habits, your relationships, your priorities, and your witness today.

1) Scripture Reading and Notes

Read each passage. Write one clear truth about living in light of the end.

1. 2 Peter 3:11 (NSV)

    ____

    ____

2. Matthew 24:44 (NSV)

    ____

    ____

3. James 4:14 (NSV)

    ____

    ____

4. 1 Peter 1:15–16 (NSV)

    ____

    ____

5. Romans 12:18 (NSV)

    ____

    ____

6. Matthew 6:19–20 (NSV)

    ____

    ____

7. Colossians 3:24 (NSV)

    ____

    ____

8. 2 Corinthians 5:10–11 (NSV)

    ____

    ____

2) Life Audit: What Matters Most

Write short answers.

1. What do you spend most of your time thinking about?

   ____

   ____

2. What do you spend most of your money on?

   ____

   ____

3. What do these patterns say about your priorities?

   ____

   ____

4. What is one priority you want to change in the next 30 days?

   ____

   ____

3) Watchfulness Plan

Matthew 24:44 calls you to be ready.

1. One habit that makes me spiritually sleepy is:

   ____

   ____

2. One habit that helps me stay ready is:

   ____

   ____

3. One change I will make this week is:

   ____

   ____

4) Holiness Step

1 Peter 1:15–16 calls believers to holiness.

1. One hidden sin I need to bring into the light is:

   ____

   ____

2. One step of repentance I will take in the next 48 hours is:

____

____

3. One boundary I will set is:

____

____

4. One replacement habit I will practice is:

____

____

5) Relationship Repair

Romans 12:18 calls you to pursue peace.

1. Is there a relationship you need to address?

____

____

2. What is one humble step you can take this week?

____

____

3. Examples: apologize, ask for a conversation, stop gossip, forgive.

____

____

4. Write one sentence you can say that is truthful and peaceful.

____

____

6) Treasure That Lasts

Matthew 6:19–20 speaks of treasure in heaven.

1. One way I will practice generosity this month is:

____

____

2. One way I will invest time in what lasts is:

____

____

3. One distraction I will reduce is:

____

____

7) Witness Step

2 Corinthians 5:10–11 speaks of persuasion in light of judgment.

1. One person I want to pray for is:

____

____

2. One way I can show love and open a door for conversation is:

____

____

3. One simple gospel sentence I can share is:

____

____

Prayer Response

Write a prayer for faithfulness. If you need help, complete these lines.
Father, teach me to live in light of the end.

____

____

Help me stay ready for Christ's return.

____

____

Strengthen me to pursue holiness and peace with others.

____

____

Help me use my time and money for what lasts.

____

____

Give me courage and love to speak the gospel with care.

____

____

Keep me faithful until the day You complete Your work.

Amen.

The end is certain, so daily faithfulness matters. Watchfulness, holiness, wise priorities, peacemaking, and humble witness are the right response to God's promised future.

CHAPTER 6

HOPE THAT NEVER FADES

Life changes fast. Health can turn overnight. Jobs can disappear. Relationships can break. Even good seasons do not last. That is why God gives a hope that does not fade. Christian hope is not wishful thinking. It is confident expectation based on God's promise and God's character.

1 Peter 1:3 says God has caused believers to be born again to a living hope through the resurrection of Jesus Christ from the dead (NSV). That verse tells us where hope comes from. It comes from new birth, and it is anchored in Christ's resurrection. Because Jesus rose, the believer's future is secure. Hope is living because Christ is living.

This hope does not depend on circumstances. It does not rise when life feels easy and collapse when life feels hard. It rests on what God has promised to do. God's promises are steady even when feelings are not.

Scripture also says this hope will not fade because it is protected by God. 1 Peter 1:5 says believers are guarded by God's power through faith for a salvation ready to be revealed (NSV). Your hope is not protected by your mood. It is protected by God's power. Faith may feel weak at times, but the One who guards you is not weak.

Hope that never fades also has content. It is not vague. It is not simply "things will work out." God tells us what we are hoping for.

We hope for the return of Christ. We hope for resurrection. We hope for the end of sin and death. We hope for God to make all things new. We hope for life with God in righteousness and joy. These hopes are not separate. They are one future held together by God's promise.

This hope is meant to shape how you live today, especially in suffering.

Romans 15:13 calls God "the God of hope" and prays that He would fill believers with joy and peace in believing, so they abound in hope by the power of the Holy Spirit (NSV). That verse teaches two important things. First, hope is connected to believing. When faith is fed, hope grows. Second, hope is strengthened by the Spirit. You are not left to create hope from nothing. God supplies it.

Hope also helps you endure hardship with patience. Romans 8:25 says if we hope for what we do not see, we wait for it with patience (NSV). Hope and patience work together. Without hope, waiting feels pointless. With hope, waiting becomes meaningful.

Hope also keeps you from giving up when you fail. Many believers fall into despair because they see their sin and weakness. They think, "I will never change." Hope answers that lie. If you belong to Christ, God will finish His work. He will complete what He began. Your growth may be slow, but your future is certain.

Hope also helps you resist sin. Sin offers short comfort with long damage. Hope offers long joy rooted in God. When you hold hope firmly, the bait of sin looks smaller. You can say no because you know what you are living for.

Hope also shapes grief. Grief is real. The Bible does not tell believers to pretend loss does not hurt. But Christian grief is different because it is not final. You can weep and still hope. You can miss a loved one and still trust God's promise. Hope does not erase tears. It keeps tears from turning into despair.

Hope that never fades also shapes how you see yourself.

Many people build identity from what they can control. When control is lost, identity collapses. But hope anchors identity in Christ. You belong to God. You are being kept. Your future is secure. That creates stability in a changing world.

Hope that never fades also protects you from cynicism.

Cynicism is the belief that nothing will change and nothing matters. Cynicism often comes from repeated disappointment. People get hurt and they stop expecting good. But Christian hope refuses to surrender to cynicism because it rests on God, not on people. People fail. God does not fail. The world breaks promises. God keeps promises.

Hope that never fades also protects you from shallow optimism.

Optimism says, "Everything will be fine." Hope says, "God will be faithful." Optimism often ignores evil. Hope looks at evil honestly and still trusts God's final victory. Hope can stand in a hospital room, at a funeral, or in persecution and still say, "God is still true, and His promises stand."

So how do you keep hope strong?

First, feed hope with Scripture. Hope grows when you remember what God has promised. When Scripture is neglected, hope often shrinks. Your mind fills with fear and noise. God's Word cuts through that.

Second, pray for hope. Romans 15:13 connects hope to prayer and to the Spirit's power. Ask God to strengthen your hope. Ask Him to help you believe. Ask Him to keep your eyes on what is coming.

Third, practice gratitude. Gratitude does not replace hope, but it supports it. When you thank God for present mercy, your heart is reminded that God is good and active even now.

Fourth, stay close to God's people. Isolation feeds despair. Fellowship strengthens hope. Other believers can remind you of truth when your own mind feels foggy.

Fifth, keep obedience connected to hope. Do not treat hope as a theory. Use hope as fuel. When you choose purity, you are choosing the future over the moment. When you forgive, you are living like the coming kingdom is real. When you serve, you are storing up treasure that lasts.

Hope that never fades is also meant to produce courage.

Hebrews 6:19 says hope is "a sure and steadfast anchor of the soul" (NSV). An anchor does not remove storms. It keeps you from drifting. When fear and pressure rise, hope holds you steady.

So what should you do when you feel hope fading?

Start by returning to Christ's resurrection. 1 Peter 1:3 roots hope there. Then name what is draining hope. Is it unconfessed sin? Is it constant fear? Is it exhaustion? Is it isolation? Bring it to God with honesty. Ask for help. Take one small step of obedience. Open Scripture. Speak with a trusted believer. Do not wait for a perfect feeling before you move. Often hope grows as you return to the means God uses.

The main point is clear. Christian hope never fades because it rests on the living Christ, the guarding power of God, and the promised future God will bring. This hope steadies suffering, strengthens patience, and fuels faithful living until the day faith becomes sight.

Workbook Section

1) Scripture Reading and Notes

Read each passage. Write one clear truth about hope.

1. 1 Peter 1:3 (NSV)

    ----

2. 1 Peter 1:5 (NSV)

    ----

3. Romans 15:13 (NSV)

    ----

4. Romans 8:25 (NSV)

    ----

5. Hebrews 6:19 (NSV)

    ----

6. Lamentations 3:21–23 (NSV)

    ----

2) Define Hope

Write a simple definition.

Christian hope means:

Now write one sentence that explains how hope is different from optimism.

Hope is different because:

----

3) Hope Drainers and Hope Feeders

Write short answers.

1.   One thing that drains my hope is:

    ----

2.   Another hope drainer is:

    ----

3.   One thing that feeds my hope is:

    ----

4.   Another hope feeder is:

Now write one change you will make this week to reduce a hope drainer.

My change:

----

4) Anchor Practice

Hebrews 6:19 calls hope an anchor.

1.   What storm are you facing right now?

    ----

2. What promise from today's passages can anchor you in that storm?

----

3. Write one sentence you will repeat when fear rises.

----

5) Waiting With Patience

Romans 8:25 links hope and patience.

1. What are you waiting for right now?

----

2. What makes waiting hard for you?

----

3. What is one faithful step you can take while you wait?

----

6) Obedience Fueled by Hope

Choose one area where you need to obey God in a hard way.

1. The obedience step is:

----

2. What fear or excuse holds you back?

----

3. How does hope in God's future help you obey today?

----

4. What is one step you will take in the next 48 hours?

Write a prayer for steady hope. If you need help, complete these lines.

Father, thank You for a living hope through the resurrection of Jesus.

When my hope feels weak, remind me that You are faithful and Your promises stand.

Guard my heart from despair and cynicism.

Fill me with joy and peace in believing by the power of Your Spirit.

Help me live faithfully while I wait for what You have promised.

Amen.

Key Takeaway

Hope that never fades is anchored in the living Christ and guarded by God's power. It steadies the soul in storms, strengthens patience in waiting, and fuels obedience until God's promises are fully seen.

CONCLUSION

HOLD THE WHOLE COUNSEL OF GOD CLOSE

You just finished a full workbook set on the big truths of the Bible: God, humanity, salvation, the Holy Spirit, and the future. These are not small topics. Yet God did not give them to confuse you. He gave them to steady you. He gave them so you can know Him, trust Him, obey Him, and endure with hope.

Systematic theology can sound like a school word. But the goal is simple. It means learning Bible truth in an ordered way, so your faith is not built on guesses. When your view of God is clear, your life becomes clearer. When your view of sin is honest, grace becomes sweeter. When your view of salvation is firm, fear loses its grip. When your view of the Spirit is biblical, you stop trying to live the Christian life alone. When your view of the future is sure, you can suffer without despair and serve without quitting.

This workbook set was written to be used, not just read. If you only read the teaching sections, you gained knowledge. But the workbook sections are where truth becomes practice. They help you slow down, name what is real, and respond to God with faith and obedience. The exercises were meant to help you build habits that last. Habits matter because you will not always feel strong. You will not always feel focused. But habits can carry you when your feelings are weak.

What you can take with you from each book

Book One helped you start where the Bible starts: with God.

You looked at God's self-revelation, His triune life, His rule over all things, His goodness, His relationship with time, and worship that is shaped by truth. This matters because every other doctrine depends on God. If you get God wrong, everything else bends. If you think God is small, you will live with small faith. If you think God is harsh, you will hide. If you think God is distant, you will stop praying. But if you know God as He has revealed Himself, you can live with reverence and peace at the same time.

A steady takeaway from Book One is this: God invites you. He is not confused, rushed, or threatened. He is worthy of trust. When life feels out of control, God is not. When you do not know what to do next, God does. Your job is not to carry the world. Your job is to obey the God who carries it.

Book Two helped you face the truth about humanity.

You saw the dignity of being made in God's image. You also faced the damage of the fall and how sin bends thinking and desire. You learned that human worth remains even after sin, and you ended with what it means to live as an image bearer today.

This matters because people often swing between pride and shame. Pride says, "I am above others." Shame says, "I am beyond hope." Both are lies. The Bible gives a better view. You are made by God, and you matter. You are also fallen, and you need mercy. That balance protects you from self-worship and self-hate at the same time.

A steady takeaway from Book Two is this: you cannot understand your life if you refuse to face sin. But you also cannot live wisely if you deny dignity. God calls you to truth and love together. That means you treat people as people, even when they sin. It also means you treat your own sin as serious, without treating yourself as worthless.

Book Three helped you grasp salvation as God's rescue.

You learned that salvation begins with God's initiative. You saw Christ's saving work. You faced the call to faith and repentance. You studied justification by faith alone. You learned what sanctification is and how it grows. You ended with assurance and endurance.

This matters because many Christians live with constant fear. They think God's love rises and falls with their performance. That creates either pride or despair. But the gospel gives a firmer foundation. Christ is enough. Your standing with God is secured by Christ, not by your mood. That does not remove the call to obedience. It places obedience in the right place. You obey because you are saved, not to earn saving.

A steady takeaway from Book Three is this: if you are in Christ, you can repent without panic. You can face sin without hiding. You can work hard at growth without trying to buy God's love. You can also rest, because your hope is not built on your record.

Book Four helped you live by the Spirit God has given.

You learned the Spirit is God, not a force. You learned the Spirit brings life, unites believers to Christ, grows fruit, builds and guides the church, and helps you walk daily.

This matters because many believers try to live the Christian life by sheer effort. Some burn out. Some pretend. Some give up. The Spirit is not an optional extra. He is God's gift for the whole Christian life. He opens eyes, strengthens obedience, grows character, and keeps the church healthy through truth and love.

A steady takeaway from Book Four is this: you do not need to chase feelings to follow God. You need truth, prayer, repentance, wise boundaries, and steady dependence. The Spirit works through ordinary faithfulness more often than sudden moments.

Book Five helped you hold fast to the future God has promised.

You learned Christ will return, the dead will be raised, heaven and hell are real and final, God will make all things new, you must live in light of the end, and hope does not fade.

This matters because many people live like this life is all there is. That produces panic, greed, and despair. But Christian hope is anchored in God's promise. The future is not fog. It is not fantasy. God will finish His work. Evil will be judged. Death will end. God will dwell with His people. This hope does not make you passive. It makes you faithful.

A steady takeaway from Book Five is this: the future makes the present meaningful. Your choices are not random. Your pain is not pointless. Your labor in the Lord is not wasted. Hope does not erase tears. It keeps tears from becoming the end of the story.

What to do now that you finished the set

It is easy to finish a workbook and move on. But the best fruit comes when you return to it. Think of this set like a tool kit. You will need it again in different seasons.

Here are practical ways to use what you learned.

1) Pick one "anchor truth" for each book

An anchor truth is a short sentence you can remember. Keep it plain. Keep it usable.

Examples you can adapt:

- **God:** "God is worthy of trust, even when I do not understand."
- **Humanity:** "People bear God's image, and sin is real."
- **Salvation:** "Christ is enough, and grace changes me."
- **Spirit:** "The Spirit helps me obey in ordinary life."
- **Future:** "God will finish what He promised, so I will be faithful today."

Write your own anchors on paper. Put them where you will see them.

2) Build a weekly rhythm that protects your faith

Many people fail because they rely on motivation. Motivation comes and goes. Rhythm is steadier.

A simple rhythm can include:

- A set time to read Scripture most days.
- One longer time each week to reflect and write.
- One time each week to gather with God's people.
- One person you can speak to with honesty.
- A plan for confession and repentance when you fall.

You do not need an impressive plan. You need a plan you will actually keep.

3) Use the workbook questions when life gets hard

Hard seasons often bring the same questions.

- "Where is God?"
- "Why do I feel numb?"
- "Why is my sin still here?"
- "Will God keep me?"
- "What is the point of staying faithful?"

When those questions rise, open this book set again. Use the questions to slow down and tell the truth. Pray in plain words. Ask for help. Take one step of obedience, not ten.

4) Study with others when possible

Some truths become clearer when you say them out loud. A small group, a spouse, a friend, or a mentor can help. You do not need a big group. Two or three can be enough.

If you study with others, keep it simple:

- Read the teaching section.
- Answer a few workbook questions.
- Share one "I learned" and one "I will do".
- Pray for each other with short prayers.

5) Keep doctrine connected to love

It is possible to learn theology and become cold. That is not the goal. Truth should grow worship, humility, and love. If learning makes you harsh, slow down and check your heart. Ask God to give you tenderness and courage together.

Truth without love becomes pride. Love without truth becomes confusion. God calls you to both.

A final reminder about growth

God does not measure growth the way people do. People notice big moments. God often grows people through small faithfulness.

Growth can look like:

- You confess sin sooner than you used to.
- You forgive faster than you used to.
- You choose restraint in speech more often.
- You pray even when you feel weak.
- You keep going after a hard week.
- You serve without needing praise.
- You stop making excuses and start taking steps.

Do not despise small growth. A tree grows quietly most days. But over time, it changes.

Also remember this: some seasons feel slow because God is doing deep work. Roots grow before fruit shows. Keep showing up. Keep repenting. Keep trusting. Keep obeying.

Copy this section. Keep it in your Bible, notebook, or on your wall. Use it daily, weekly, and monthly. If you miss a day, do not quit. Start again.

Daily Checklist: 10 minutes that steady your soul

- I read a portion of Scripture today.
- I asked God for help in plain words.
- I named one temptation I faced and brought it into the light.
- I took one small step of obedience.
- I thanked God for one clear mercy today.
- I spoke words that build, not words that tear down.
- I chose one boundary that protects my mind or body.
- I asked, "How can I love someone today?" and I acted on it.

Daily Heart Check: quick questions

- Did I treat God as real today, or as distant?
- Did I trust my feelings more than God's truth today?
- Did I hide sin, or confess it?
- Did I use people, or serve people?
- Did I spend time on what lasts, or mostly on what fades?

Weekly Checklist: set your direction again

- I gathered with a local church or a faithful group of believers.
- I reviewed one chapter's workbook pages from any book in this set.
- I wrote one confession and one request for help.
- I encouraged one believer with a message, call, or visit.
- I served in a practical way, even if it felt small.
- I gave time or money to support God's work as I am able.
- I rested in a wise way, without guilt and without laziness.
- I made peace where I could, by speaking or forgiving.

Weekly Doctrine Check: keep the foundations firm

- God is holy, good, and worthy of trust.
- People bear God's image and have real dignity.

- Sin is real and it damages the heart.
- Salvation is by grace through faith in Christ.
- I am justified by faith, not by works.
- The Spirit is God and He helps me obey.
- Christ will return, and God will judge and renew all things.
- My hope is anchored in God's promise, not my mood.

Monthly Checklist: deeper review and repair

- I chose one sin pattern to confront with a clear plan.
- I set or renewed one wise boundary (time, media, spending, speech).
- I had one honest talk with a mature believer about my walk with God.
- I reviewed my use of time and adjusted one habit that wastes it.
- I checked my relationships and took one step toward peace or repair.
- I served someone who cannot repay me.
- I re-read one full book introduction and one chapter that I need most.
- I prayed for someone who does not know Christ.

Crisis Checklist: when you feel weak, numb, or afraid

- I stopped and admitted what I feel without pretending.
- I asked, "What is true about God right now?" and wrote one sentence.
- I confessed any known sin, without excuses.
- I reached out to one trusted believer for prayer or help.
- I took one small step of obedience today, not ten.
- I rested if I am exhausted.
- I remembered the promised future and refused despair.

One-Page Commitment: sign and date

Write this in your own words, then sign it.

- I will seek God in Scripture and prayer with steady habits.
- I will take sin seriously and repent quickly.

- I will trust Christ's finished work when guilt rises.
- I will depend on the Holy Spirit for daily obedience.
- I will stay connected to the church and serve with humility.
- I will live in light of Christ's return with hope and faithfulness.

Signature: _______________________

Date: _______________________

Final encouragement

If you are trusting Christ, you are not alone. God is with you. He has spoken. He has saved. He has given His Spirit. He has promised a future that will not fail. The goal now is not to become impressive. The goal is to be faithful.

Keep returning to God's Word. Keep praying in plain speech. Keep repenting when you sin. Keep loving your neighbor. Keep serving the church. Keep your hope anchored in what God has promised.

And when you feel tired, remember this: the God who began His work in you does not quit halfway. He will finish what He has started.

APPENDIX
BIBLE STUDY PLANS AND MEMORY WORK

This appendix turns the whole 5-in-1 workbook into a simple program you can repeat. It is built for real life. It uses short readings, clear prompts, and small next steps.

Important note: **This appendix lists Scripture references only.** It does not print any Bible verses.

PART 1: HOW TO STUDY THE BIBLE IN FOUR STEPS

Use these four steps every time you read.

Step 1: Observe

Ask: **What does it say?**

- o   Who is speaking?
- o   Who is listening?
- o   What happens?
- o   What words repeat?
- o   What command is given?
- o   What promise is given?

Write 2–3 facts you can point to in the passage.

Step 2: Understand

Ask: **What does it mean?**

- o   What is the main point?
- o   What does this teach about God?
- o   What does this teach about people?
- o   What does this show about sin or grace?

Write one short sentence: "This passage means ..."

Step 3: Apply

Ask: **What should I do?**

- o   What sin should I confess?
- o   What truth should I believe?
- o   What habit should I start?
- o   What habit should I stop?
- o   Who should I love or serve?

Write one action step you can do in 24–48 hours.

Step 4: Pray

Ask: **What should I ask God for?**

Pray in simple words:

- o   Praise: "God, You are..."
- o   Confess: "I have..."
- o   Ask: "Please help me..."
- o   Thanks: "Thank You for..."

PART 2: 10-WEEK BIBLE READING PLAN (50 READINGS)

Plan: 5 days per week (Monday–Friday).

Weekend: review your notes and answer the weekly questions.

Each day includes:

- Read (NSV reference)
- Notice (2 questions)
- Do (1 action)
- Pray (1 prompt)
- One-sentence summary

Week 1: Know God as He Has Revealed Himself

Day 1 (Mon) Read: Exodus 34:6–7

Notice: What does God say about Himself? What do you learn about mercy and justice?

Do: Write one reason you can trust God today.

Pray: Ask God to help you believe His name is good.

Summary: God tells the truth about who He is.

Day 2 (Tue) Read: Deuteronomy 6:4–5

Notice: What does God command? What does love look like here?

Do: Choose one time today to speak love for God out loud.

Pray: Ask God to unite your heart to love Him.

Summary: God calls for whole-heart love.

Day 3 (Wed) Read: Isaiah 55:8–9

Notice: How are God's ways different from ours? What does this correct in you?

Do: Write one area where you will stop demanding your own way.

Pray: Ask for humility to accept God's wisdom.

Summary: God is higher than our plans.

Day 4 (Thu) Read: Psalm 145:8–9

Notice: What words describe God's heart? Who receives His care?

Do: Show patience to one person today.

Pray: Thank God for His steady compassion.

Summary: God's kindness reaches far.

Day 5 (Fri) Read: John 17:3

Notice: What is eternal life in this verse? What does it say about knowing God?

Do: Write one sentence that defines eternal life in plain words.

Pray: Ask God to help you know Him truly.

Summary: Life is found in knowing God.

Weekend Review (No new reading)

- What truth about God was most clear this week?

- What did you learn about trusting Him?

- What is one habit you want to keep next week?

Day 6 (Mon) Read: Matthew 3:16–17

Notice: Who is present in this scene? What does the Father say?

Do: Write three short lines: Father, Son, Spirit. What does each do here?

Pray: Praise God for His unity and love.

Summary: God is one, and God is three persons.

Day 7 (Tue) Read: Matthew 28:18–20

Notice: What authority does Jesus claim? What name are disciples baptized into?

Do: Write one step to obey Jesus this week.

Pray: Ask for courage to follow Christ's command.

Summary: The triune name stands over the church.

Day 8 (Wed) Read: John 14:16–17

Notice: What does Jesus promise? What does this teach about the Spirit?

Do: Write one area where you need help and comfort.

Pray: Ask God to strengthen you by His Spirit.

Summary: The Spirit is given to help and stay.

Day 9 (Thu) Read: 2 Corinthians 13:14

Notice: What gift is named from each person of the Trinity?

Do: Write one sentence of thanks for grace, love, and fellowship.

Pray: Thank God for His care in three persons.

Summary: God's blessings flow from Father, Son, and Spirit.

Day 10 (Fri) Read: Ephesians 1:3–5

Notice: What does the Father plan? What does this show about His love?

Do: Write one fear you will answer with God's adoption love.

Pray: Thank the Father for choosing to bless His people.

Summary: The Father's plan is loving and sure.

Weekend Review (No new reading)

- What part of the Trinity teaching was new to you?

- How does it change prayer?

- What is one way to honor God with your worship?

Week 3: Recognize God's Sovereignty in All Things

Day 11 (Mon) Read: Daniel 4:34–35

Notice: Who rules? What does this say about human power?

Do: Hand one worry to God in writing.

Pray: Tell God you trust His rule.

Summary: God's rule cannot be stopped.

Day 12 (Tue) Read: Proverbs 19:21

Notice: What do people plan? What finally stands?

Do: List your plans for the week, then write "God is Lord" below them.

Pray: Ask for peace with God's will.

Summary: God's purpose holds.

Day 13 (Wed) Read: Psalm 115:3

Notice: Where is God? What does He do?

Do: Say one sentence today: "God can do what He pleases."

Pray: Ask God to shape your desires to match His.

Summary: God is free and able.

Day 14 (Thu) Read: Isaiah 46:9–10

Notice: What does God declare? What does He promise to do?

Do: Write one promise from this passage in your own words.

Pray: Praise God for His sure plan.

Summary: God's plan stands from start to end.

Day 15 (Fri) Read: Romans 11:36

Notice: Where do all things come from? What is the right response?

Do: Write one sentence of worship that gives God glory.

Pray: Praise God for His greatness.

Summary: All things are from God and for God.

Weekend Review (No new reading)

- Where did you see God's rule in your week?

- What did you learn about control?

- What will you do next week when plans change?

Week 4: Trust God's Moral Goodness

Day 16 (Mon) Read: Psalm 34:8

Notice: What is the invitation? What is the result of trusting?

Do: Write one way you will "taste" God's goodness today (obedience choice).

Pray: Ask God to help you trust His goodness.

Summary: God invites trust, not fear.

Day 17 (Tue) Read: Nahum 1:7

Notice: What is God like? Who does He know?

Do: Write your name next to "those who take refuge."

Pray: Ask God to be your safe place today.

Summary: God is a safe refuge.

Day 18 (Wed) Read: James 1:17

Notice: What comes from God? What does this say about His character?

Do: List three good gifts you received this week.

Pray: Thank God for steady goodness.

Summary: God gives what is good.

Day 19 (Thu) Read: Psalm 86:5

Notice: What does God give? Who can call on Him?

Do: Make one honest request to God today.

Pray: Ask God to help you come without shame.

Summary: God is ready to forgive.

Day 20 (Fri) Read: Romans 8:32

Notice: What did God give? What does that prove?

Do: Write one fear, then write "God did not spare His Son" beside it.

Pray: Thank God for love shown in Christ.

Summary: The cross proves God's goodness.

Weekend Review (No new reading)

- Where do you doubt God's goodness most?

- What truth helped you this week?

- What will you do when you feel bitterness rise?

Week 5: Understand God's Relationship with Time

Day 21 (Mon) Read: Psalm 90:1–2

Notice: How long has God been God? What does that mean for you?

Do: Write one worry you will place under God's eternal care.

Pray: Praise God for being everlasting.

Summary: God is before all time.

Day 22 (Tue) Read: 2 Peter 3:8–9

Notice: How does God view time? What does this show about patience?

Do: Write one place where you need patience today.

Pray: Thank God for His patience with sinners.

Summary: God is patient and purposeful.

Day 23 (Wed) Read: Ecclesiastes 3:1

Notice: What does this say about seasons? How does that comfort you?

Do: Name your current season in one word.

Pray: Ask God for wisdom in your season.

Summary: God orders seasons.

Day 24 (Thu) Read: Isaiah 40:28

Notice: What does God never do? What does that mean for your weak days?

Do: Write one sentence: "God does not grow tired."

Pray: Ask God to give strength today.

Summary: God is never worn out.

Day 25 (Fri) Read: Revelation 1:8

Notice: What titles does God claim? What does that say about His control?

Do: Write "He is" at the top of a page, then list what God is.

Pray: Praise God as the beginning and the end.

Summary: God holds all time.

Weekend Review (No new reading)

- What changed in your view of time?

- What does patience look like for you?

- What is one habit that helps you live wisely in your days?

Week 6: Worship God in Truth

Day 26 (Mon) Read: John 4:23–24

Notice: What kind of worshipers does God seek? What must worship include?

Do: Write one way you will worship today in truth (not just feeling).

Pray: Ask God to help you worship with a true heart.

Summary: Worship must be true and Spirit-shaped.

Day 27 (Tue) Read: Psalm 96:9

Notice: What does it mean to worship in holy splendor?

Do: Remove one distraction for your next prayer time.

Pray: Ask God for reverence.

Summary: Worship calls for reverence.

Day 28 (Wed) Read: Hebrews 12:28–29

Notice: What kind of worship is fitting? What does it say about God?

Do: Write one sentence of gratitude for God's kingdom.

Pray: Ask for a thankful, careful heart.

Summary: God is holy and worthy.

Day 29 (Thu) Read: Colossians 3:17

Notice: What does "in the name of the Lord Jesus" cover?

Do: Pick one task today and do it as worship.

Pray: Ask God to shape your daily life as worship.

Summary: All of life can honor Christ.

Day 30 (Fri) Read: Psalm 100:4–5

Notice: What actions are commanded? What reason is given?

Do: Write a short list of thanks (5 items).

Pray: Thank God for His steadfast love.

Summary: Gratitude is part of worship.

Weekend Review (No new reading)

- What makes your worship shallow?

- What makes your worship steadier?

- What is one change you will keep?

Day 31 (Mon) Read: Genesis 1:27

Notice: What does this say about God's image? What does it say about male and female?

Do: Write one way you will honor human dignity today.

Pray: Ask God to help you treat people with honor.

Summary: Humans bear God's image.

Day 32 (Tue) Read: Genesis 3:6–7

Notice: What choice is made? What is the first result?

Do: Write one lie you are tempted to believe.

Pray: Ask God to help you trust His word.

Summary: Sin brings shame and hiding.

Day 33 (Wed) Read: Romans 3:23

Notice: Who has sinned? What do we lack?

Do: Write one area you need God's mercy.

Pray: Confess sin plainly.

Summary: All need grace.

Day 34 (Thu) Read: Jeremiah 17:9–10

Notice: What is the heart like? What does God do?

Do: Ask God to search one motive in you.

Pray: Ask for a clean heart.

Summary: God sees deeper than we do.

Day 35 (Fri) Read: Psalm 51:10

Notice: What does David ask for? What does that show about change?

Do: Write one request for inner change, not just outer change.

Pray: Ask God for renewal.

Summary: God can renew the heart.

Weekend Review (No new reading)

- What did you learn about dignity and sin?

- What is one habit that helps you fight hiding?

- What is one way to show honor to others?

Week 8: Grasp Salvation in Christ

Day 36 (Mon) Read: Ephesians 2:4–5

Notice: What moves God to act? What does He give?

Do: Write one sentence: "God made me alive by grace."

Pray: Thank God for mercy.

Summary: Salvation comes from God's mercy.

Day 37 (Tue) Read: Romans 5:1

Notice: What do we have through faith? Who gives it?

Do: Write one fear that peace with God answers.

Pray: Thank God for peace through Christ.

Summary: Faith brings peace with God.

Day 38 (Wed) Read: Acts 4:12

Notice: Where is salvation found? What is excluded?

Do: Write the name "Jesus" and circle it.

Pray: Thank God for a sure Savior.

Summary: Salvation is in Christ alone.

Day 39 (Thu) Read: 2 Corinthians 5:17

Notice: What changes in Christ? What becomes new?

Do: Write one "old" pattern you want to leave behind.

Pray: Ask God to grow new life in you.

Summary: In Christ, new life begins.

Day 40 (Fri) Read: Romans 8:1

Notice: What is removed? Who is this for?

Do: Write one sentence to answer guilt today.

Pray: Thank God for no condemnation in Christ.

Summary: Condemnation is removed for those in Christ.

Weekend Review (No new reading)

- What part of salvation teaching helped most?

- What part is still hard to believe?

  ____

  ____

- What will you do when guilt rises?

  ____

  ____

Week 9: Live by the Spirit God Has Given

Day 41 (Mon) Read: Acts 5:3–4

Notice: Who is the Spirit called? What does that teach?

____

____

Do: Write one sentence that honors the Spirit as God.

____

____

Pray: Ask for a reverent heart.

____

____

Summary: The Spirit is God.

____

____

Day 42 (Tue) Read: Titus 3:5–6

Notice: Who renews? What does God pour out?

____

____

Do: Write one area where you need renewal.

____

____

Pray: Ask God for renewal by the Spirit.

____

____

Summary: The Spirit brings new life.

Day 43 (Wed) Read: Romans 8:9

Notice: What marks belonging to Christ?

Do: Write one reason to be grateful if you belong to Christ.

Pray: Thank God for His presence in you.

Summary: The Spirit marks God's people.

Day 44 (Thu) Read: Galatians 5:22–23

Notice: What fruit is named? Which fruit do you need most now?

Do: Choose one fruit to practice today.

Pray: Ask the Spirit to grow it in you.

Summary: The Spirit grows Christlike character.

Day 45 (Fri) Read: 1 Corinthians 12:7

Notice: Why are gifts given? Who benefits?

Do: Plan one act of service this week.

Pray: Ask God to help you build up others.

Summary: Gifts are for the common good.

Weekend Review (No new reading)

- Where do you depend on self instead of the Spirit?

- What fruit do you want to grow next week?

- How can you serve the church in a small way?

Week 10: Hold Fast to the Future God Has Promised

Day 46 (Mon) Read: Acts 1:11

Notice: What promise is given? What does it say about Jesus returning?

Do: Write one sentence of readiness: "I will live ready."

Pray: Ask God to keep you watchful.

Summary: Jesus will return.

Day 47 (Tue) Read: 1 Corinthians 15:52

Notice: What happens at the last trumpet? What changes?

Do: Write one fear of death, then write "God will raise the dead."

Pray: Ask God for courage.

Summary: Resurrection is real.

Day 48 (Wed) Read: Matthew 25:46

Notice: What two outcomes are named? What does "eternal" teach?

Do: Pray for one person who needs Christ.

Pray: Ask God to give mercy and repentance.

Summary: Eternity is final.

Day 49 (Thu) Read: Revelation 21:5

Notice: Who speaks? What promise is made?

Do: Write one broken thing you long to see made new.

Pray: Ask God to keep your hope steady.

Summary: God will make all things new.

Day 50 (Fri) Read: Hebrews 6:19

Notice: What is hope compared to? What does an anchor do?

Do: Write one promise you will cling to this week.

Pray: Ask God to anchor your soul.

Summary: Hope holds you steady.

Final Weekend Review (No new reading)

- What truth from the whole plan mattered most to you?

- What changed in your habits?

- What do you want to repeat in the next 10 weeks?

PART 3: SCRIPTURE MEMORY PATH

How to use this

- Write the verse reference on a card.

- Write the first letter of each word (or write the verse in your own notebook).

- Say it out loud once a day for 5 days.

- Review older verses every week.

Week 1	Week 2
1. Psalm 23:1	6. John 1:14
2. Isaiah 26:3	7. Hebrews 1:3
3. Proverbs 3:5–6	8. Colossians 1:15–16
4. Psalm 46:10	9. John 14:6
5. Deuteronomy 31:8	10. Philippians 2:10–11

Week 3

11. Psalm 103:8
12. Lamentations 3:22–23
13. Numbers 23:19
14. 1 Samuel 2:2
15. Psalm 118:24

Week 4

16. Genesis 2:7
17. Psalm 8:4–5
18. Job 33:4
19. Ecclesiastes 7:20
20. Proverbs 4:23

Week 5

21. John 3:16
22. Romans 6:23
23. 1 Timothy 1:15
24. Isaiah 1:18
25. Acts 3:19

Week 6

26. Romans 10:13
27. John 6:37
28. Ephesians 1:7
29. 2 Corinthians 5:21
30. Hebrews 9:27–28

Week 7

31. James 1:22
32. Micah 6:8
33. Colossians 3:12
34. 1 Peter 2:9
35. Matthew 5:16

Week 8

36. Galatians 2:20
37. Romans 8:14
38. Zechariah 4:6
39. 2 Timothy 1:7
40. 1 Corinthians 6:19–20

Week 9

41. Matthew 6:33
42. Luke 9:23
43. 1 Thessalonians 5:16–18
44. Proverbs 15:1
45. Hebrews 10:24

Week 10

46. John 14:3
47. 1 Thessalonians 4:16
48. Revelation 22:12
49. 2 Peter 3:13
50. Romans 15:13

PART 4: TROUBLESHOOTING PAGES (WHEN YOU FEEL STUCK)

These pages are short on purpose. Use them when you feel stuck. Read the references, then answer the prompts.

A) If You Feel Spiritually Dry

Read (NSV): Psalm 63:1–2; Isaiah 41:10; John 7:37–39

- What do you want from God right now?

- What is one thing you are avoiding: prayer, Scripture, confession, church?

- What is one small step you can take today, not later?

- Who can pray with you this week?

- Prayer prompt: Ask God for fresh desire and steady faith.

B) If You Feel Crushed by Guilt

Read (NSV): Psalm 32:1–2; 1 John 1:9; Hebrews 4:16

- What sin do you need to confess plainly?

- What makes you want to hide?

- What does it mean to come to God with confidence?

- What is one repair step you need to take with another person?

- Prayer prompt: Confess, then thank God for forgiveness in Christ.

C) If You Feel Stuck in Temptation

Read (NSV): 1 Corinthians 10:13; Matthew 26:41; Psalm 119:9

- What is your most common trigger?

- What lie does temptation tell you?

- What "way of escape" can you take right now?

- What boundary will you set for the next 7 days?

- Prayer prompt: Ask God for a clear mind and strength to obey.

D) If You Feel Angry at God

Read (NSV): Psalm 13:1–2; Job 1:21; Romans 11:33

- What loss or pain is under your anger?

- What do you wish God would change?

- What is one truth you can hold even while you hurt?

- Who can listen and pray with you without judging you?

- Prayer prompt: Tell God the truth, then ask Him to help you trust Him.

E) If You Feel Anxious About the Future

Read (NSV): Matthew 6:34; Philippians 4:6–7; Psalm 121:1–2

- What is your biggest fear right now?

- What is one thing you can do today that is wise and simple?

- What is one thing you need to release because you cannot control it?

- What is one promise you can repeat this week?

- Prayer prompt: Ask God for peace and a steady mind.

PART 5: PRINT-AND-KEEP TRACKING PAGES

10-Week Progress Tracker

Check one box each day you complete.

Week 1

Mon	[ ]
Tue	[ ]
Wed	[ ]
Thu	[ ]
Fri	[ ]
Weekend Review	[ ]

Week 2

Mon	[ ]
Tue	[ ]
Wed	[ ]
Thu	[ ]
Fri	[ ]
Weekend Review	[ ]

Week 3

Mon	[ ]
Tue	[ ]
Wed	[ ]
Thu	[ ]
Fri	[ ]
Weekend Review	[ ]

Week 4

Mon	[ ]
Tue	[ ]
Wed	[ ]
Thu	[ ]
Fri	[ ]
Weekend Review	[ ]

Week 5

Mon	[ ]
Tue	[ ]
Wed	[ ]
Thu	[ ]
Fri	[ ]
Weekend Review	[ ]

Week 6

Mon	[ ]
Tue	[ ]
Wed	[ ]
Thu	[ ]
Fri	[ ]
Weekend Review	[ ]

<table>
<tr><td colspan="2">Week 7</td><td colspan="2">Week 8</td></tr>
<tr><td>Mon</td><td>[ ]</td><td>Mon</td><td>[ ]</td></tr>
<tr><td>Tue</td><td>[ ]</td><td>Tue</td><td>[ ]</td></tr>
<tr><td>Wed</td><td>[ ]</td><td>Wed</td><td>[ ]</td></tr>
<tr><td>Thu</td><td>[ ]</td><td>Thu</td><td>[ ]</td></tr>
<tr><td>Fri</td><td>[ ]</td><td>Fri</td><td>[ ]</td></tr>
<tr><td>Weekend Review</td><td>[ ]</td><td>Weekend Review</td><td>[ ]</td></tr>
<tr><td colspan="2">Week 9</td><td colspan="2">Week 10</td></tr>
<tr><td>Mon</td><td>[ ]</td><td>Mon</td><td>[ ]</td></tr>
<tr><td>Tue</td><td>[ ]</td><td>Tue</td><td>[ ]</td></tr>
<tr><td>Wed</td><td>[ ]</td><td>Wed</td><td>[ ]</td></tr>
<tr><td>Thu</td><td>[ ]</td><td>Thu</td><td>[ ]</td></tr>
<tr><td>Fri</td><td>[ ]</td><td>Fri</td><td>[ ]</td></tr>
<tr><td>Weekend Review</td><td>[ ]</td><td>Weekend Review</td><td>[ ]</td></tr>
</table>

Memory Tracker (50 references)

Check each one when you can say it from memory.

1. .... [ ]	26. .... [ ]
2. .... [ ]	27. .... [ ]
3. .... [ ]	28. .... [ ]
4. .... [ ]	29. .... [ ]
5. .... [ ]	30. .... [ ]
6. .... [ ]	31. .... [ ]
7. .... [ ]	32. .... [ ]
8. .... [ ]	33. .... [ ]
9. .... [ ]	34. .... [ ]
10. .... [ ]	35. .... [ ]
11. .... [ ]	36. .... [ ]
12. .... [ ]	37. .... [ ]
13. .... [ ]	38. .... [ ]
14. .... [ ]	39. .... [ ]
15. .... [ ]	40. .... [ ]
16. .... [ ]	41. .... [ ]
17. .... [ ]	42. .... [ ]
18. .... [ ]	43. .... [ ]
19. .... [ ]	44. .... [ ]
20. .... [ ]	45. .... [ ]
21. .... [ ]	46. .... [ ]
22. .... [ ]	47. .... [ ]
23. .... [ ]	48. .... [ ]
24. .... [ ]	49. .... [ ]
25. .... [ ]	50. .... [ ]

Week 1

Big truth I learned: _______________________________________

One sin to confess or resist: _______________________________

One person to love or serve: _______________________________

One step I will take in 48 hours: ____________________________

Prayer request: ____

Week 2

Big truth I learned: _______________________________________

One sin to confess or resist: _______________________________

One person to love or serve: _______________________________

One step I will take in 48 hours: ____________________________

Prayer request: ____

Week 3

Big truth I learned: _______________________________________

One sin to confess or resist: _______________________________

One person to love or serve: _______________________________

One step I will take in 48 hours: ____________________________

Prayer request: ____

Week 4

Big truth I learned: _______________________________________

One sin to confess or resist: _______________________________

One person to love or serve: _______________________________

One step I will take in 48 hours: ____________________________

Prayer request: ____

Week 5

Big truth I learned: ___________________________________

One sin to confess or resist: ___________________________

One person to love or serve: ___________________________

One step I will take in 48 hours: _______________________

Prayer request: _______________________________________

Week 6

Big truth I learned: ___________________________________

One sin to confess or resist: ___________________________

One person to love or serve: ___________________________

One step I will take in 48 hours: _______________________

Prayer request: _______________________________________

Week 7

Big truth I learned: ___________________________________

One sin to confess or resist: ___________________________

One person to love or serve: ___________________________

One step I will take in 48 hours: _______________________

Prayer request: _______________________________________

Week 8

Big truth I learned: ___________________________________

One sin to confess or resist: ___________________________

One person to love or serve: ___________________________

One step I will take in 48 hours: _______________________

Prayer request: _______________________________________

Week 9

Big truth I learned: _______________________________________

One sin to confess or resist: _______________________________

One person to love or serve: _______________________________

One step I will take in 48 hours: ___________________________

Prayer request: ____

Week 10

Big truth I learned: _______________________________________

One sin to confess or resist: _______________________________

One person to love or serve: _______________________________

One step I will take in 48 hours: ___________________________

Prayer request: ____

HERE'S ANOTHER BOOK BY JAMES NORTHWELL THAT YOU MIGHT LIKE